Frerè's Chess Hand-book

Jno. B. Carpenter
Longstreet, 1862

FRERÈ'S
CHESS HAND-BOOK.

CONTAINING

ELEMENTARY INSTRUCTION AND THE LAWS OF CHESS,

TOGETHER WITH

FIFTY SELECT GAMES,

BY THE FIRST PLAYERS.

ENDINGS OF GAMES.

AND THE

DEFEAT OF THE MUZIO GAMBIT.

ALSO, THIRTY-ONE OF THE CHOICEST CHESS PROBLEMS, AND A
DESCRIPTION OF, AND RULES FOR,

FOUR-HANDED CHESS.

BY THOMAS FRÈRE.

NEW YORK:
L. W. STRONG 98 NASSAU STREET.
1858.

ENTERED according to Act of Congress, in the year 1858.
By THOMAS W. STRONG,
In the Clerk's Office of the District Court of the United States,
for the Southern District of New York.

PREFACE.

————•◦•————

THE extraordinary increase in the number of Chess Amateurs, throughout the United States, during the past year,
has induced the publisher to issue, in separate form, the arti-
cle on Chess, from his book of general games published last
year.

It may not be uninteresting to the lovers of the fascinat-
ing game, to consider here, briefly, the causes which have
produced such pleasing effects, as a wide diffusion of a taste
for their favorite pastime. The movement primarily grew
out of the almost accidental meeting of a few players at
"Limberger's," in the city of New York. During the latter
part of the year 1854 might be seen, on any afternoon, from
one to three o'clock, at an unknown saloon corner of Fulton
and Nassau streets, two gentlemen playing at Chess. The
board was about ten inches square, and broken in two pieces,

the pieces being laid together on the table, and adjusted from
time to time, as the peculiar violence of one of the players
would drive things all awry. The men were of the large club
size, and in a. lamentably delapidated condition, and of such
dimensions that when they were placed upon the pieces of
the little leather board they were crowding, upsetting, and
jostling each other in the most lively manner. There were
usually the two players and one looker-on. The brave remarks and terrible style of one of the players at first misled
the observer, who scarcely knew the moves, leading him to believe that the unfortunate quiet French gentleman was about
to be most mercilessly used up and reduced, in fact, pulver-
ized to the extremity of nothingness. But the looker-on very
soon discovered that the quiet French gentleman not only
gave the odds of the Rook, but won all the games. The dashing brave, from the fair land of Poland, never *did*, but always
was to win. The quiet French gentleman was Mr. Bally, his
opponent was Mr. Keller, and the looker-on was the writer
of this sketch

Shortly after this commencement of public Chess playing,
Mr. Limberger was induced, not only to replace the misera-
ble little leather board with a new and larger one, but also
to provide more boards and men.

Soon new players began to appear; and, in something

like the following rotation, during 1855, they took their places at the boards. Möhle, Schultz, Roberts, Eschwege, Wilhelmi, Schuffner, Channing, Hamilton and others. The writer very well remembers the afternoon on which a certain distinguish-ed player made his first appearance. An argument was being had on a Pawn end-game, as to whether or not the game could be drawn. A quiet, gentlemanly, pleasant-speaking young man, an entire stranger, sitting at the table, suggested that the game could be drawn. A small wager of refresh-ments was proposed to the stranger that the game could not be drawn, which wager was quietly accepted, and after a few moves the game *was* clearly drawn. The stranger was Lich-tenhein, (now President of the New York Chess Club,) and the victim, Frère.

During the year 1856, and following close upon the *debut* of Mr. Lichtenhein, came Fuller, Marache, Dr. Raphael, Col. Mead, King, Thompson, T. L. Loyd, S. Loyd, Perrin, Stanley, Dodge, Horner, Weekes, Montgomery, Philip, Pelham, Knott, Ayres, Dr. Schmidt of Cincinnati; Mr. Ferguson of Lockport; Judge Meek of Alabama; Julien, Tolman, Jee, Wheelwright, Reif, Quimby, Howells, Eidlitz, Kind, Schmidt of Brooklyn; Fiske, Oscanyan, Hines, Freidrichs, Hazeltine, Cooper, Byrne, Woolfe, Beeman, Carples, Pollack, Rice, Dr. McNulty, Sweet, Keyser, Paine, Clark and many others. The following year

1857, gave an additional number of promising amateurs, but no players of note. Among others were Fletcher, Croley, Hicks, Crawford, Hinde, Freidrichs the younger, Hall, Gillet, Tilton and others.

The effect of this public playing was to increase very sensibly the number of members of the New York and the Brooklyn Chess clubs.—This increase, in its turn, suggested to the minds of Messrs. Fiske, Miller and Hazeltine, the idea of publishing the "Chess Monthly," which idea was carried out by the issue of No. 1, of that excellent periodical in January 1857. For the idea of the "National Chess Congress," and Grand National Chess Tournament, the American public is indebted to the Editors of the "Monthly," who believed it practicable to carry out an undertaking similar to that so successfully carried out at "The World's Chess Tournament" at London in 1851.

With the history of "The First American Chess Congress" the reader is undoubtedly familiar. If not, he should procure the "Book of the Congress" at once.

Lastly.—The immediate cause of the astonishing spread of a taste for the game in this country was the "Chess Congress," supported as it was by the matchless skill of Murphy and the impurturbable, impenetrable, boundless brain of Paul-

men, who has accomplished, with unqualified success, the astounding task of playing TEN games, all at once, without the sight either of boards or men.

Hoping this little book may "remunerate" all who may make "an investment" in it, the writer dismisses the subject

T. F.

N. Y. JUNE, 1858.

CONTENTS.

FRÈRE'S CHESS HAND-BOOK.

Elementary Instruction.

CHESS is played by two players, on the ordinary chequered board of sixty-four squares, each player having sixteen Chess-men under his control, of a different color to those of his antagonist. The Chess-men consist of eight pieces and eight pawns on each side, namely:

The King.	The Queen.	Two Rooks.	Two Bishops.	Two Knights.	Eight Pawns.

At the commencement of the game, the board is placed with a white corner at the right-hand side, and the men are arranged as on the following diagram:

THE BLACK MEN.

THE WHITE MEN.

The better way for the learner to become familiar with the moves of the Chess-men, is to request some one acquainted with the game to teach them to him. They move as follows:

The pawn, at its first move, has the privilege of going one square forward or two squares, as may be deemed most advantageous by the player. But after the first move of each pawn, then it can only advance one square at a move. The pawn can never move backward, but becomes a queen, or any other piece, on reaching its eighth square of the board. The pawn captures other pawns or pieces by moving one square *diagonally*, and cannot capture by moving forward, nor can it move diagonally except in capturing.

The bishop moves only diagonally, and for any distance both backward and forward that may happen to be unincumbered, and captures wherever it has a right to move. The bishops never change from squares of one color to the squares of the other color, but always run on the color on which they are placed at the commencement of the game. The white king's bishop always runs on white squares; the white queen's bishop always runs on black squares; the black king's bishop always runs on black squares, and the black queen's bishop always runs on white squares.

The rook (sometimes called the castle) runs any distance forward, backward, or sideways, but never diagonally, and captures wherever it has a right to move.

The queen simply has the move both of the bishop and the rook; it can, therefore, move any distance forward, backward, sideways, or diagonally, and captures wherever it has a right to move.

The king moves but one square, and can go either diagonally, forward, backward, or sideways. Consequently it can move on any square that joins or touches the square on which it stands, and captures as it moves.

The move of the knight can scarcely be understood without verbal explanations. However, some one of several different modes of stating the same thing may strike the mind of the learner so as to be understood. First, the knight moves to the opposite corner of every six squares, lying together three by three, from that corner of the six that he may occupy when about to move. Second, which states the same thing in another manner: the knight goes one square forward or backward and then two squares side-ways; or, *vice versa*, one square sideways and two squares backward or forward. The following diagram shows the move of the knight. The white knight in the centre can move to any of the eight black squares numbered, not-withstanding he is so closely encircled by other men.

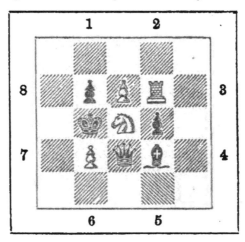

No piece, except the knight, can, in moving, pass over either their own colored men, or the men of the opposite color. The pieces can capture the pieces or pawns of the opposite color, and take them off from any squares, where the moving piece may have a right to go. The pawns capture only diagonally, as before stated.

The king can never be taken. But the whole object of the game is to get your opponent's king in such a position that he may be taken without your antagonist having any resource left to extricate him. When this is the case, the game is ended. This predicament is called *checkmate*, the accomplishment of which is the grand object of both the combatants. If the king is only *attacked*, and has a re-source to extricate himself, the attacking party must give notice by saying "check." See laws of the game, No. 18.

There is a compound move of the king and rook allowed once in each game, to each player, called castling, and is performed thus: suppose that on the king's side the bishop and knight have been moved out, then the king could be moved to the knight's square, and the king's castle brought around and placed on the king's bishop's square. Also on the queen's side—suppose the queen, queen's bishop, and queen's knight have been played out of the way, then the king could cross one square, and occupy queen's bishop's square, and the castle could be moved to queen's square. For further instruction as to castling, see laws of the game, No. 16.

There is a move of the pawn which may be termed irregular, and is called "*taking en passant*," or taking in passing. This move is sufficiently explained by laws of the game, No. 15, to which the reader is referred.

TECHNICAL TERMS USED IN THE GAME OF CHESS.

Pieces.—The eight superior men on each side are technically called *pieces* in contradistinction to the *pawns.*

Notation.—Notation is the mode adopted to describe the various moves in recording games, openings of games, situations, problems, endings of games, &c. The squares of the chess-board take their names from the pieces occupying them at the beginning of the game. Thus we say "king's square," king's 2nd square, king's 3rd square, and so on to king's 8th square. The same with the other pieces—we say king's knight's square, and so on to king's knight's 8th square. The pieces on the king's side are king's bishop, king's knight, and king's rook; on the queen's side the pieces are the queen, the queen's bishop, queen's knight, and queen's rook; so that all the squares of the chess-board take their names from the original position of the pieces, each file being numbered up to the 8th square. The same rule holds good with both players. Therefore white king's 5th square is black king's 4th square; so white queen's 7th square is black queen's 2nd square; and so on for every piece and every square. The abbreviations used in recording games, &c., are as follows:

K. for king.	Kt. for knight.
Q. for queen.	P. for pawn.
R. for rook.	Sq. for square.
B. for bishop.	Ch. for check.

Consequently, instead of writing out the moves in full, they are recorded as follows—the moves being numbered for convenience of reference:

1. P. to K.'s 4th . . . . .for pawn to king's fourth square.
2. K. Kt. to B.'s 3rd . . . . . .for king's knight to bishop's third square.
3. K. B. to Q. B.'s 4th . . . . for king's bishop to queen's bishop's fourth square.

The word square is used only in speaking of a piece's own square; as K.'s sq., Q.'s sq., K. B.'s sq., Q. Kt.'s sq., &c.

In moving pawns we sometimes say, for instance, K. P. 2, or K. P. 1, instead of saying P. to K.'s 4th, or P. to K.'s 3rd. We may say in any stage of the game such or such a pawn 1, which means advancing the pawn particularized one square.

Doubled pawn.—Two pawns on one file are called a doubled pawn.

Rank.—The word *rank* is used in contradistinction to the word *file.* The first rank of squares is the row occupied by the pieces at the commencement of the game. The second rank is that occupied by the pawns, and so on to the eighth rank. White's first rank is black's eighth rank, &c. The word file means the rows of squares running the other way of the board, from one player to the other, and are named after the various pieces occupying them before a move is made. There are the K.'s file, Q.'s file, K. B.'s file, Q. B.'s file, K. Kt.'s file, Q. Kt.'s file, K. R.'s file, and Q. R.'s file. The names of the files being the same with both players.

Stalemate.—Is when the king of one of the players is so situated that he cannot move it without going into check, and at the same time has no other move on the board.

Drawn game.—There are several ways to make a drawn game. 1st. Stalemate is a drawn game. 2nd. When one of the players has such a position that he can perpetually "check" his adversary, and insists on doing so. 3rd. When there is not sufficient power remaining on the board to give checkmate. 4th. When both players insist on making the same move respectively, neither being willing to change his mode of play. See also laws of the game, Nos. 22, 23, and 24.

En prise.—When a piece or pawn is so placed that it may be captured, it is said to be *en prise.*

The exchange.—One player is said to gain the exchange of another when he succeeds in exchanging a bishop or a knight for a rook. The latter being considered the more valuable piece.

False move.—A move made contrary to the rules of the game.

20*

Forced move.—A move which must be made, before any other, by press of circumstances.

To interpose—Is to play a piece or pawn between the attacking power and the attacked.

Isolated pawn—Is a lone pawn without other pawns on the files next on either side.

J'adoube—Is a French expression signifying "I arrange," "I adjust," or, "I replace." See *Laws of the game*, Nos. 7 and 9.

Gambit—Is an Italian word, and signifies "tripped up." It is used to distinguish a particular class of openings of games from another class called "close" games.

Close game—Is a game commenced without the sacrifice of a pawn, in contradistinction to "Gambit," which requires such sacrifice.

Minor pieces.—The bishops and knights are sometimes called *minor pieces*, as they are inferior in value to the queen and rook.

The opposition.—That player is said to have the opposition whose king is opposite to the other king, with only one square between them, and his opponent being compelled to move.

Party or *Partie.*—Sometimes used instead of the word "game."

Passed pawn—Is a pawn which has passed through all obstruction of the opponent's pawns.

Perpetual check—Is when one player has it in his power to continue checking his opponent's king without the possibility of being prevented doing so.

Pion coiffé or *Marked pawn.*—A pawn with which a superior player agrees to checkmate his adversary.

Queening a pawn.—See *Laws of the game*, No. 21.

Discovered check.—A check uncovered by the removal of a pawn or piece.

Smothered mate—Is checkmate given with the knight, when the mated king is completely blocked by pieces or pawns of his own, or of his opponent, so that he cannot be moved.

Fool's mate—Is checkmate in two moves, as follows:

WHITE.	BLACK.
1. K. Kt.'s P. to K. Kt.'s 4th.	1. K. P. to K.'s 4th.
2. K. B. P. to K. B.'s 4th.	2. Q. to K. R.'s 5th checkmate.

Scholar's mate—Is checkmate in four moves, as follows:

WHITE.	BLACK.
1. P. to K.'s 4th.	1. P. to K.'s 4th.
2. K. B. to Q. B.'s 4th.	2. K. B. to Q. B.'s 4th.
3. Q. to K. R.'s 5th.	3. Q. P. to Q.'s 3rd.
4. Q. takes K. B. P. checkmate.	

Relative value of the pieces.—The relative value of the pieces is estimated as follows: the Queen is worth, say, 10 pawns; the Rook 5; the Bishop $3\frac{1}{2}$; the Knight $3\frac{1}{4}$.

LAWS OF THE GAME,

Adopted by the London Chess Club upon its establishment in 1807; recently revised by the Committee of that Institution. Sanctioned, also, and adopted by the New York and the Brooklyn Chess Clubs.

1. The chess-board must be so placed that each player has a white corner square nearest his right hand. If the board have been improperly placed, it must be adjusted, provided *four* moves on each side have not been played, but not afterwards.

2. If a piece or pawn be misplaced at the beginning of the game, either player may insist upon the mistake being rectified, if he discover it before playing his fourth move, but not afterwards.

3. Should a player, at the commencement of the game, omit to place all his men on the board, he may correct the omission before playing his fourth move, but not afterwards.

4. If a player, undertaking to give the odds of a piece or pawn, neglect to remove it from the board, his adversary, after four moves have been played on each side, has the choice of proceeding with, or recommencing the game.

5. When no odds are given, the players must take the first move of each game alternately, drawing lots to determine who shall begin the first game. If a game be drawn, the player who began it has the first move of the following one.

6. The player who gives odds has the right of moving first in each game, unless otherwise agreed. Whenever a pawn is given, it is understood to be always the king's bishop's pawn.

7. A piece or pawn touched must be played, unless at

the moment of touching it, the player say "*J'adoube*," or words to that effect; but if a piece or pawn be displaced or overturned by accident, it may be restored to its place.

Note to No. 7, by George Walker.

Nothing can be easier than to acquire the habit of saying "*J'adoube*," when necessary, and a little reflection will convince you of the propriety of following, to the strictest letter of the law, a rule which prevents persons of careless habits from touching half-a-dozen pieces by turns, or all at once, before making their move. Indeed, were it not for this law, I believe some people, while calculating their move, would take off a rook or two to play with.

D is to move, and lifts a bishop, with the evident intention of setting it on a certain square; then replaces it, saying, "J'adoube," and proceeds to play elsewhere. He certainly *should* play elsewhere, for he should not play with me. The bishop must of course be moved. *The expression " J'adoube" is not allowed to exonerate you when you touch a piece, with the bona fide intention of moving it.*

8. While a player holds the piece or pawn he has touched, he may play it to any other than the square he took it from; but having quitted it, he cannot recall the move.

9. Should a player touch one of his adversary's pieces or pawns, without saying "*J'adoube*," or words to that effect, his adversary may compel him to take it; but if it cannot be legally taken, he may oblige him to move the king: should his king, however, be so posted that he cannot be legally moved, no penalty can be inflicted.

10. Should a player move one of his adversary's men, his antagonist has the option of compelling him, 1st, to replace the piece or pawn and move his king; 2nd, to replace the piece or pawn and take it; 3rd, to let the piece or pawn remain on the square to which it had been played, as if the move were correct.

11. If a player takes one of his adversary's men with one of his own that cannot take it without making a false move, his antagonist has the option of compelling him to take it with a piece or pawn that can legally take it, or to move his own piece or pawn which he touched.

12. Should a player take one of his own men with another, his adversary has the option of obliging him to move either.

13. If a player make a false move, *i. e.*, play a piece or pawn to any square to which it 'cannot legally be moved, his adversary has the choice of three penalties, viz.: 1st, of compelling him to let the piece or pawn remain on the square to which he played it; 2nd, to move it correctly to another square; 3rd, to replace the piece or pawn and move his king.

14. Should a player move out of his turn, his adversary may choose whether both moves shall remain, or the second be retracted.

15. When a pawn is first moved in a game, it may be played one or two squares; but in the latter case the opponent has the privilege of taking it *en passant* with any pawn which could have taken it had it been played one square only. A pawn cannot be taken *en passant* by a piece.

16. A player cannot castle in the following cases: 1st. If the king or rook have been moved. 2nd. If the king be in check. 3rd. If there be any piece between the king and rook. 4th. If the king pass over any space attacked by one of the adversary's pieces or pawns.

Should a player castle in any of the above cases, his adversary has the choice of three penalties, viz.: 1st, of insisting that the move remain; 2nd, of compelling him to move the king; 3rd, of compelling him to move the rook.

17. If a player touch a piece or pawn that cannot be moved without leaving the king in check, he must replace the piece or pawn and move his king; but if the king cannot be moved, no penalty can be inflicted.

18. If a player attack the adverse king without saying "check," his adversary is not obliged to attend to it; but, if the former, in playing his next move, were to say "check," each player must retract his last move, and he that is under check must obviate it.

19. If the king has been in check for several moves, and it cannot be ascertained how it occurred, the player whose king is in check must retract his last move, and free his king from the check; but if the moves made subsequent to the check be known, they must be retracted.

20. Should a player say "check" without giving it, and his adversary in consequence move his king, or touch a piece or pawn to interpose, he may retract such move, provided his adversary have not completed his next move.

21. Every pawn which has reached the eighth or last square of the chess-board, must be immediately exchanged for a queen or any other piece the player may think fit, even though all the pieces remain on the board. It follows, therefore, that he may have two or more queens, three or more rooks, bishops, or knights.

22. If a player remain at the end of the game, with a rook and bishop against a rook; with both bishops only; with knight and bishop only, etc., he must checkmate his adversary in fifty moves on each side at most, or the game will be considered as drawn; the fifty moves commence from the time the adversary gives notice that he will count them. This law holds good for all other checkmates of pieces only, such as queen or rook only, queen against a rook, etc., etc.

23. If a player agree to checkmate with a particular piece or pawn, or on a particular square, or engage to force his adversary to stalemate or checkmate him, he is not restricted to any number of moves.

24. A stalemate is a drawn game.

25. If a player make a false move, castle improperly, etc., etc., the adversary must take notice of such irregularity before he touches a piece or pawn, or he will not be allowed to inflict any penalty.

26. Should any question arise respecting which there is no law, or in case of a dispute respecting any law, the players must refer the point to the most skilful and disinterested bystanders, and their decision must be considered as conclusive.

FRÈRE'S CHESS MAXIMS

For the practice of those Amateurs who are ambitious of becoming really fine players.

1. Never allow yourself to play what is commonly called a "quick game."

2. Always play strictly according to the acknowledged rules, and require your opponent to do likewise.

8. Equalize all games, as nearly as possible, by taking or giving odds.

4. When you receive the odds of the "rook" or "knight," from a strong player, change off the pieces and pawns at every fitting opportunity; placing your dependence on

winning the game by "the ending;" at the same time watching an opportunity to sacrifice the "piece," and force checkmate. But if you receive the odds of the pawn and two moves, or the pawn and one move, then play to maintain the attack and force the game.

5. If an adversary is possessed with the idea that he is the stronger player, and you hold a contrary opinion, offer to play for a " consideration," to decide the matter.

6. When your opponent is so unreasonable as to decline taking proper odds, bring the " consideration" test to bear upon him also.

7. Never underrate, in your own mind, an adversary's strength, but endeavor to consider every game you play *an equal match*, and govern yourself accordingly.

8. *Play always to win*, desiring " quarter" from no one, nor giving any.

9. Never allow an advantage gained to influence you to play carelessly, but finish off the game in the most direct and masterly manner possible, unless your opponent elects, of his own free will, to resign.

10. Do not allow a trifling loss or disadvantage to alarm you, but remember that a game is neither lost nor won until the final checkmate.

11. When there is obviously a good move for you, search the board for a *better one* before you play.

12. Do not allow your opponent's remarks, or violent manner of moving, to disconcert you; or some, even inferior, players will frighten you out of the game.

13. If you are satisfied that you cannot win the game, turn your attention to drawing it; but do not be so unwise as to inform your adversary of your intention.

14. Do not be too ready to resign, because "the ending" is generally the most instructive part of the game.

15. When you are a "looker on," never, under any circumstances, make remarks in relation to the game, unless appealed to by the players, nor lose your temper when others interfere in your own game, but merely enter a good-natured protest against a continuance of the interruption.

16. When asked how you play, in comparison with others, underrate your own game rather than the reverse, as you thereby divest yourself of much responsibility, and can better afford to be beaten.

17. Never give it out that you can "beat" so-and-so, but leave him and others to find it out for themselves.

18. "Last, though not least"—Never allow success nor defeat to influence your manner, but, *at all times, practise the utmost imperturbation.*

MAXIMS FOR BEGINNERS;

And General Observations.

It is a good general practice to castle early in the game, and on the king's side.

If the queens have been exchanged before castling, it is generally better to move the king than to castle.

It is often bad play to take an adversary's pawn if it is so placed as to give protection to your king.

Employ the king in active play towards the ending of the game.

It is generally better to cover a check to your king with a piece that attacks the checking power than with one that does not.

It is usually good play to force your adversary's king into the centre of the board, that you may more effectually bring your pieces to bear upon him.

Do not give useless checks to your adversary's king, as you thereby lose moves.

It is mostly bad play to bring out your queen in the early stages of the game, as you thereby expose her to attacks from your opponent's inferior forces.

It is not always good play to capture a pawn, or even a piece, with your queen, if by so doing you isolate her too much from the rest of your game.

It is commonly good play to prevent your opponent from castling.

Bring your rooks into play as soon as possible, and with them take possession of the open files.

A rook on your adversary's second rank, if his king be not moved out, is usually well posted.

Moving your queen's pawn to queen's third before moving your king's bishop, is apt to confine your bishop and crowd your game.

The bishops impede the onward march of the pawns more than knights or rooks. Profit by this suggestion through exchanges, when you are strong in pawns, at the ending of the game.

It is not good play to move the knights on the rook's files, as their strength is thereby greatly curtailed.

Towards the ending of a game, the knight is generally stronger than a bishop, provided the pawns on both sides are equal.

Be careful not to allow a knight to attack your king and an undefended piece at the same time, as the latter would be lost.

Do not allow a protected pawn to attack, or "fork," two of your pieces.

If possible, keep command of the centre of the board with your pawns.

Doubled pawns are usually disadvantageous.

United pawns are strong, but they lose much of their strength when separated.

A passed pawn is valuable, especially when supported by another pawn.

Play your pieces so that they will not interfere with, but support, each other.

If a violent attack is brought to bear upon you, play to exchange pieces.

Do not allow yourself to acquire a choice of men. Accustom yourself to play with either color.

Bring all your pieces as speedily into action as possible, and endeavor to crowd your adversary's game; remembering that, to prevent his doing that which you are endeavoring to do yourself, will eventually prove to your advantage.

ON GIVING AND RECEIVING ODDS.

When there exists a disparity of skill, it is usual for the stronger player to give his adversary such odds as will render the game mutually interesting, by placing the parties more strictly on terms of equality. I earnestly recommend beginners never to engage with players of known superiority, without asking for proper odds. It is not fair to insist on better players engaging on even terms; since, in that case, what may be amusing enough to you, will probably to them prove a positive annoyance, the chances of victory being so unfairly balanced.

The first description of odds, worthy of notice, is the

queen; for, until you can make a stand, with the advantage allowed you of this great piece, you can hardly be said to know the moves. The player giving the queen you will find mostly to aim at a quiet opening. On your part, endeavor to get all your pieces out, and your king snugly castled, before you do aught else; and remember that, as "exchanging" is death to your opponent, you must seek every opportunity to exchange your pieces for his; with a due regard, in so doing, to the scale of relative value, and to a cautious examination of the consequences, as far as you can calculate.

The odds of "the marked pawn," are about equal to the queen. The parties have each the usual complement of men; but the superior player puts a ring, or some other mark, on a certain pawn, and undertakes to give checkmate with that pawn only. If he give mate with any piece, or with any other pawn, he loses; and he is not permitted to queen the marked pawn, but must give the mate with it, *as a pawn*.

The odds of the rook and knight stand next in the scale; and you may be said to be a very fair player, as players go, when a first-rate player can only make even games in giving you these two pieces. The odds of the two knights will be substituted, as you improve, for the advantage of the rook and knight.

The odds of the rook mark the boundary line between "The world" and the "Chess-circle." The latter is more confined than you would suppose, there not being fifty persons in London to whom the first-rate player could not give a rook. All such trials of skill should consist of not less than eleven games; and he who wins, on the average, six out of the eleven, may fairly say he can give the odds in question, whatever they may be. Indeed, without you could insure winning seven or eight games out of eleven, I should not allow that you had fairly got over the rook. It is absurd to suppose, as I have heard it asserted, that the rook is not so much to give as the knight, because it cannot so speedily be brought into play. Those accustomed to allow large odds well know the difference. In giving the rook, unless a violent attack is soon concocted, the game becomes highly critical; and you can frequently get a fine position by sacrificing one of your rooks for a minor piece; but it is seldom you can do this, receiving the knight.

The odds of the knight follow the rook. The strongest opening, in giving the knight, is Captain Evans's game. You may diminish the odds of the knight, by receiving either that piece, or the rook, in exchange for the pawn with one or more moves.

The pawn and three moves, the pawn and two moves, and the pawn and move, are the lighter odds; and are allowed between players nearly matched, according as they are found to answer in rendering the game equal.—*Geo. Walker.*

PRELIMINARY GAME.
(From Staunton's Hand-book.)

Preparatory to the investigation of the several openings treated of in the following pages, it may not be uninstructive to give a short game which shall exhibit the application of some technical phrases in use at Chess, and at the same time show a few of the most prominent errors into which an inexperienced player is likely to fall.

In this game, the reader will be supposed to play the white pieces and to have the first move; although, as it has been before remarked, it is advisable for you to accustom yourself to play with either black or white, for which purpose it is well to practise the attack, first with the white and then with the black pieces.

WHITE.	BLACK.
1. K.'s P. to K.'s 4th.	1. K.'s P. to K.'s 4th.

When the men are first arranged in battle order, it is seen that the only pieces which have the power of moving are the knights, and that to liberate the others it is indispensably necessary to move a pawn. Now, as the king's pawn, on being moved, gives freedom both to the queen and to the king's bishop, it is more frequently played at the beginning of the game than any other. You will remember, in speaking of the pawns it was shown that on certain conditions they have the privilege of going either one or two steps when they are first moved.

2. K.'s B. to Q. B.'s 4th.	2. K.'s B. to Q. B.'s 4th.

Thus far the game illustrative of the *king's bishop's* opening is correctly begun. Each party plays his king's bishop thus, because it attacks the most vulnerable point of the adverse position, viz., the *king's bishop's pawn.*

| 3. Q. B.'s pawn to B.'s 3rd. | 3. Q.'s knight to B.'s 3rd. |

In playing this pawn, your object is afterwards to play queen's pawn to queen's 4th square, and thus establish your pawns in the centre; but black foresees the intention, and thinks to prevent its execution by bringing another piece to bear upon the square.

| 4. Q.'s pawn to Q.'s 4th. | 4. Pawn takes Q.'s pawn. |
| 5. Q. B.'s pawn takes pawn. | 5. K.'s B. takes pawn. |

Here you have played without due consideration. Black's third move of queen's knight to bishop's 3rd square was a bad one, and afforded you an opportunity of gaining a striking advantage; but omitting this, you have enabled him to gain a valuable pawn for nothing. Observe, now, your reply to his third move was good enough (4. Queen's pawn to queen's 4th square), but when he took your pawn with his, instead of taking again, you ought to have taken his *king's bishop's pawn* with your bishop, giving check: the game would then most probably have gone on thus:

5. *K.'s B. takes K. B.'s pawn* (ch.)	5. *K. takes bishop.*
6. *Queen to K. R.'s 5th* (ch.)	6. *K. to his B.'s square.*
7. *Queen takes K.'s bishop* (ch.)	

In this variation, you see black has lost his king's bishop's pawn, and, what is worse, *has lost his privilege of castling*, by being forced to move his king; and although for a moment he had gained a bishop for a pawn, it was quite clear that he must lose a bishop in return by the check of the adverse queen at king's rook's 5th square. It is true that he need not have taken the bishop, but still his king must have moved, and white could then have taken the king's knight with his bishop, having always the better position.

But now to proceed with the actual game:

| 6. K.'s knight to K. B.'s 3rd. | 6. Queen to K. B.'s 3rd. |

Bringing out the knight is good play; you not only threaten to win his bishop, but you afford yourself an opportunity of castling whenever it may be needful. Black would have played better in retiring the bishop from the attack to queen's knight's 3rd square, than in supporting it with the queen.

| 7. Knight takes bishop. | 7. Queen takes knight. |

Both parties played well in their last moves. You rightly took off the bishop, because supported by the queen he

menaced your queen's knight's pawn, and black properly
retook with his queen instead of the knight, because having a pawn ahead, it was his interest to exchange off the
queens.

8. Q.'s knight to Q.'s 2nd.   8. K.'s knight to B.'s 3rd.

You played correctly here in not exchanging queens, and
also in protecting your bishop and your king's pawn, both
of which were attacked by the adverse queen; but all this
might have been done without impeding the movements
of any of your pieces, by simply playing queen to king's
2nd square; as it is, the knight entirely shuts your queen's
bishop from the field. Black properly brings another piece
to the attack of your king's pawn:

9. K. B.'s pawn to B.'s 3rd.   9. Q.'s knight to king's 4th.

In protecting the king's pawn with your king's bishop's
pawn, you are guilty of a very common error among young
players; as you improve, you will find that it is rarely
good play to move the king's bishop's pawn to the third
square: in the present instance, for example, you have de-
prived yourself of the power of castling, at least for some
time, since the adverse queen now commands the very
square upon which your king, in castling on his own side,
has to move. Black's last move is much more sensible.
He again attacks your bishop, and by the same move
brings his queen's knight into co-operation with the king's
on the weak point of your position:

10. Pawn to Q. Kt.'s 3rd.   10. Q. takes queen's rook.

This is a serious blunder indeed. In your anxiety to save
the threatened bishop, which you feared to withdraw to
Q. Kt.'s 3rd square on account of the adverse knight's giving check at your queen's third square, you have actually
left your queen's rook *en prise!* Black takes it, of course,
and having gained such an important advantage, ought to
win easily.

11. Castles (*i. e.* plays K. to his Kt.'s   11. Q.'s Kt. takes bishop.
     sq., and R. to K. B.'s sq.)
12. Kt. takes Kt.   12. Castles.
13. Q. to her 2nd.   13. Q. B.'s pawn to B.'s 4th.

Your last move is very subtle; finding the mistake that
black had committed in not retreating his queen directly
after winning the rook, you determine, if possible, to prevent her escape by gaining command of all the squares she

can move to. Seeing the danger, black throws forward this pawn to enable him, if possible, to bring the queen off, by playing her to her 5th square, giving check.

14. Bishop to Q. Kt.'s 2nd.   14. Q. takes Q. R.'s pawn.

This move of the bishop is well timed: it does not, to be sure, prevent the queen from escaping for a move or two, but it gives you an attack, and very great command of the field.

15. Q. to K. Kt.'s 5th.   15. Knight to K.'s square.

Very well played on both sides. By playing the queen to K. Kt.'s 5th, you threatened to win his knight by at once taking it with your bishop, which he could not retake without opening check on his king. Instead of so moving, you might have played the knight to queen's rook's 5th square; in which case, by afterwards moving the rook to queen's rook's square, it would have been impossible for his queen to get away.

16. Q. to king's 3rd.   16. K. R.'s pawn to R.'s 3rd.

You prudently retreated your queen to guard her knight's pawn, which it was important to save, on account of its protection to the knight. Black played the king R.'s pawn to prevent your queen returning to the same post or attack.

17. K. R.'s P. to R.'s 3rd.   17. K. to his R.'s sq.

Here are two instances of what is called "lost time" at chess, neither move serving in the slightest degree to advance the game of the player. That you should have overlooked the opportunity of gaining the adverse queen was to be expected. Similar advantages present themselves in every game between young players, and are unobserved.

18. K. B.'s pawn to B.'s 4th.   18. Q. Kt.'s pawn to Kt.'s 3rd.

Again you have failed to see a most important move; you might have taken the K. rook's pawn with your queen, giving check safely, because black could not take your queen without being in check with your bishop. All this time, too, your opponent omits to see the jeopardy his queen is in, and that as far as practical assistance to his other pieces is concerned, she might as well be off the board.

19. K. Kt.'s pawn to Kt.'s 4th.   19. Q. Kt.'s pawn to Q. Kt.'s 4th.

Your last move is far from good. By thus attacking your

knight, black threatens to win a piece, because upon playing away the knight you must leave the bishop unprotected.

20. Pawn to K. Kt.'s 5th.	20. Pawn takes knight.

Although your knight was thus attacked, it might have been saved very easily. In the first place, by your taking the adversary's Q. B.'s pawn, threatening to take his king's rook, on his removing which, or interposing the Q.'s pawn, you could have taken the pawn which attacked your knight; or, in the second place, by moving your queen to her 2nd square. In the latter case, if black ventured to take the knight, you would have won his queen by taking the K. Kt.'s pawn with your bishop, giving check, and thus exposing his queen to yours. Black would have been obliged to parry the check, either by taking the bishop or removing his king, and you would then have taken his queen. This position is very instructive, and merits attentive examination.

21. B. to Q. B'.s 3rd.	21. Pawn takes Q. Kt.'s pawn.
22. Pawn to K. R.'s 4th.	22. Pawn to Q. Kt.'s 7th.

In such a position, the advance of your king's flank pawns is a process too dilatory to be very effective.

28. Pawn to K. B.'s 5th.	23. Pawn to Q. Kt.'s 8th, becoming a queen.

Now the fault of your tortoise-like movements with the pawns becomes fatally evident. Black has been enabled to make a second queen, and has an overwhelming force at command.

24. Rook takes queen.	24. Queen takes rook (check).

You had no better move than to take the newly-elected queen, for two queens must have proved irresistible.

25. King to his Kt.'s 2nd.	25. Kt. to queen's 3rd.
26. K. Kt.'s pawn to Kt.'s 6th.	26. P. takes pawn.
27. P. takes pawn.	27. Bishop to Q. Kt.'s 2nd.

Here you have given another remarkable instance of lost opportunity. At your last move you might have redeemed all former disasters by checkmating your opponent in two moves. Endeavor to find out how this was to be accomplished.

28. K. R.'s pawn to R.'s 5th.	28. Knight takes king's pawn.
29. Bishop to king's 5th.	29. Kt. to K. Kt.'s 4th (discovering check).

Up to black's last move you had still the opportunity of winning the game as before mentioned.

30. King to Kt.'s 3rd.	30. K.'s rook to B.'s 6th (ch.)
31. King to R.'s 4th.	31. Q. to K. bishop's 4th.

At this point you were utterly at the mercy of your antagonist, but fortunately he wanted the skill to avail himself properly of his vast superiority in force and position, or he might have won the game in half a dozen different ways.

32. Q. takes rook.	32. Q. takes queen.
33. B. takes K. Kt.'s pawn (ch.)	33. King takes bishop.

This was your last chance, and its success should serve to convince you that in the most apparently hopeless situations of the game there is often a latent resource, if we will only have the patience to search it out. By taking the bishop, black has left your king, *who is not in check*, no move without going into check, and as you have neither piece nor pawn besides to play, you are *stalemated*, and the game is *drawn*.

----◆----

Games

ACTUALLY PLAYED BY THE FINEST PLAYERS.

In order to condense as much solid chess information and amusement as possible in the space allotted us, we shall give entire games, with the name of the opening in which each is played, rather than the mere opening. The learner may therefore follow the game through the opening only, or to the end, as he sees fit.

We shall give the games without many notes or extended comment, believing the learner will derive more benefit by trying to discover the object of the various moves, than he would were every one to be explained to him, to say nothing of the increased pleasure of making the discovery for one's self.

THE GIUOCO PIANO OR "ROYAL OPENING."

WHITE. Mr. Mongredien.   **BLACK. Herr Anderssen.**

WHITE. Mr. Mongredien.	BLACK. Herr Anderssen.
1. K. P. 2.	1. K. P. 2.
2. K. Kt. to B.'s 3rd.	2. Q. Kt. to B.'s 3rd.
3. B. to Q. B.'s 4th.	3. B. to Q. B.'s 4th.
4. Q. B. P. 1.	4. K. Kt. to B.'s 3rd.
5. Q. P. 2.	5. P. takes P.
6. P. takes P.	6. B. to Q. Kt.'s 5th (ch.)
7. B. to Q.'s 2nd.	7. B. takes B. (ch.)
8. Kt. takes B.	8. Q. P. 2.
9. P. takes P.	9. Kt. takes P.
10. Castles.	10. Castles.
11. B. takes Kt. (a)	11. Q. takes B.
12. Q. to Q. Kt.'s 3rd.	12. Q. to K. R.'s 4th.
13. Q. Kt. to K.'s 4th.	13. B. to K.'s 3rd.
14. Q. to Q. B.'s 3rd.	14. K. B. P. 2.
15. Q. to Q. B.'s 5th.	15. Q. R. to Q.'s square.
16. Q. Kt. to Q. B.'s 3rd. (b)	16. K. R. to K. B.'s 3rd.
17. Q. P. 1.	17. K. B. P. 1.
18. K. R. to K.'s square.	18. B. to K. B.'s 2nd.
19. Q. to Q. Kt.'s 5th.	19. R. to K. Kt. 3rd.
20. K. to K. R.'s square.	20. R. takes K. Kt. P. (c)
21. Q. to Q.'s 3rd.	21. Q. to K. R.'s 6th.
22. Q. to K.'s 4th.	22. B. to K. R.'s 4th.
23. Q. takes B. P.	23. B. takes Kt.
24. R. to K.'s 3rd.	24. R. to Kt.'s 8th (ch.)

And wins.

(a) This is not commendable, for, besides bringing the adverse Q. into play, he has now great difficulty to defend his Q. P.

(b) We should have preferred playing Q. Kt. to K. Kt.'s 3rd or 5th.

(c) A very brilliant sacrifice, and one which we believe to be perfectly sound. The variations arising from K. takes R. are too numerous to allow of our giving them; but we invite our readers to a careful examination of this most interesting position, and we can promise that they will be amply rewarded for their time and trouble.

THE KNIGHT'S GAME OF RUY LOPEZ.

BLACK. Capt. Kennedy.   **WHITE. Mr. Lowenthal.**

BLACK. Capt. Kennedy.	WHITE. Mr. Lowenthal.
1. K. P. 2.	1. K. P. 2.
2. K. Kt. to B.'s 3rd.	2. Q. Kt. to B.'s 3rd.
3. K. B. to Q. Kt.'s 5th.	3. K. B. to B.'s 4th.
4. Q. B. P. 1.	4. K. Kt. to K.'s 2nd.
5. Castles. (a)	5. Castles.
6. Q. P. 2.	6. P. takes P.
7. P. takes P.	7. B. to Q. Kt.'s 3rd.
8. Q. P. 1.	8. Q. Kt. to Kt.'s square.
9. Q. P. 1.	9. P. takes P.
10. Q. takes P.	10. Kt. to K. Kt.'s 3rd.
11. Q. Kt. to B.'s 3rd.	11. Q. Kt. to B.'s 3rd.
12. Q. Kt. to Q.'s 5th.	12. Q. R. P. 1.
13. K. B. to R.'s 4th. (b)	13. B. to R.'s 2nd.
14. Q. B. to K.'s 3rd.	14. B. to Q. Kt.'s square.
15. Q. to Q. R.'s 3rd.	15. Q. Kt. P. 2.
16. K. B. to Kt.'s 3rd.	16. Q. R. P. 1.
17. Q. to B.'s 5th.	17. K. B. to R.'s 2nd.

18. Q. to Q.'s 6th. (c)	18. B. takes B.
19. P. takes B.	19. Q. R. P. 1.
20. B. to Q. B.'s 2nd.	20. Q. R. to R.'s 3rd.
21. Q. to K. Kt.'s 3rd.	21. B. to Kt.'s 2nd.
22. Q. R. to Q.'s square.	22. Q. Kt. to K.'s 2nd.
23. K. Kt. to Kt.'s 5th.	23. K. B. P. 1.
24. Kt. takes R.'s P. (d)	24. K. takes Kt.
25. Kt. takes Kt.	25. Q. takes Kt.
26. Q. to K. R.'s 3rd (ch.)	26. K. to Kt's square.
27. Q. R. takes P.	27. Q. to B's 4th.
28. R. takes B.	28. Kt. to K.'s 4th. (e)
29. Q. to K. Kt.'s 3rd.	29. K. R. to B.'s 2nd.
30. R. takes R.	30. K. takes R.
31. B. to Q.'s square.	31. R. to Q.'s 3rd.
32. B. to K. R.'s 5th (ch.)	32. K. Kt. P. 1.
33. B. to K.'s 2nd.	33. R. to Q.'s 7th.
34. Q. to K. B.'s 4th. (f)	34. R. takes B.
35. Q. takes K. B.'s P. (ch.)	35. K. to K.'s square.
36. Q. to K.'s 6th (ch.)	36. K. to Q.'s square.
37. Q. to K. Kt.'s 8th (ch.)	37. K. to Q. B.'s 2nd.
38. Q. to K. Kt.'s 7th (ch.)	38. Kt. to Q.'s 2nd.
39. R. to Q.'s square.	

White mated in three moves.

(a) Q. P. 2nd at once is rather more attacking.

(b) We should have preferred retiring this B. to B's. 4th, and if White then played K. B. to R.'s 2nd, move Q. B. to K. Kt.'s 5th.

(c) It is obvious that taking the Q. Kt. P. would have lost the "exchange."

(d) Very well played.

(e) If White had now taken B. with Q., his opponent would have played Q. to Q.'s 7th, with a forced won game.

(f) This sacrifice is not sound.

IRREGULAR OPENING,

Played at the Brooklyn Chess-club, between the Secretary, Mr. T. Frère, and Mr. W. Horner.

BLACK. Mr. Frère.	WHITE. Mr. Horner.
1. P. to Q. B.'s 4th.	1. P. to K.'s 4th.
2. P. to K.'s 3rd.	2. P. to K. B.'s 4th.
3. P. to Q. R.'s 3rd.	3. Kt. to K. B.'s 3rd.
4. Kt. to Q. B.'s 3rd.	4. P. to Q. B.'s 4th.
5. P. to Q.'s 3rd.	5. Kt. to Q. B.'s 3rd.
6. Kt. to K. B.'s 3rd.	6. P. to Q.'s 3rd.
7. B. to K.'s 2nd.	7. B. to K.'s 3rd.
8. Castles.	8. B. to K.'s 2nd.
9. P. to Q. Kt's 3rd.	9. Castles.
10. B. to Q. Kt.'s 2nd.	10. R. to Q. B.'s sq.
11. P. to K. R.'s 3rd.	11. Q. to Q.'s 2nd.
12. Kt. to K. Kt.'s 5th.	12. Q. Kt. to Q.'s sq.
13. P. to K. B.'s 4th.	13. P. to K. R.'s 3rd.
14. Kt. takes B.	14. Q. takes Kt.
15. P. takes P.	15. P. takes P.
16. Q. to Q. B.'s 2nd.	16. Kt. to K. B.'s 2nd.
17. B. to K. B.'s 3rd.	17. Kt. to Q.'s 3rd.
18. Kt. to Q.'s 5th.	18. P. to K.'s 5th.
19. P. takes P.	19. Q. Kt. takes P.
20. B. takes Kt.	20. Kt. takes B.

21. Kt. to K. B.'s 4th.	21. Q. to K. B.'s 2nd.
22. B. to K.'s 5th.	22. B. to K. B.'s 3rd.
23. B. takes B.	23. Q. takes B.
24. Kt. to Q.'s 5th.	24. Q. to K.'s 4th.
25. Q. R. to Q.'s sq.	25. Q. R. to Q. B.'s 3rd.
26. Q. R. to Q.'s 3rd.	26. Q. R. to K. Kt.'s 3rd.
27. Kt. to K. B.'s 4th.	27. Q. R. to K. B.'s 3rd.
28. Q. R. to Q.'s 5th.	28. Q. to K.'s sq.
29. K. R. to Q.'s sq.	29. P. to K. Kt.'s 4th.
30. R. to Q.'s 8th.	30. Q. to K.'s 4th.
31. R. takes R. (ch.)	31. R. takes R.
32. Kt. to Kt.'s 6th.	32. Q. to K. Kt.'s 6th.
33. Kt. to K.'s 7th (ch.) (*a*)	33. K. to R.'s 2nd.
34. Kt. takes P. (*b*)	34. Q. to K.'s 4th.
35. R. to Q.'s 7th (ch.)	35. K. to R.'s sq.
36. R. to K.'s 7th.	36. Q. takes Kt.
37. R. takes Kt.	37. P. to Q. Kt.'s 3rd.
38. Q. to Q.'s 3rd.	38. P. to K. R.'s 4th.
39. Q. to Q. B.'s 3rd (ch.)	39. K. to Kt.'s sq.
40. R. to K.'s 7th.	40. R. to K. B.'s 2nd.
41. R. to K.'s 8th (ch.)	41. K. to R.'s 2nd.

And black mates in three moves.

(*a*) Taking the rook would subject him to a strong counter attack.
(*b*) The correct move.

Note.—The leading players of the Brooklyn Chess-club are Messrs. Daniel S. Roberts, W. Horner, J. Philip, William Kind, C. W. Shuffner, F. Schmidt, Worthington Hines, and Frère.

BISHOP'S GAMBIT.

Brilliant game between Herr Erkel and Herr Szen.

WHITE. Herr Erkel.	BLACK. Herr Szen
1. P. to K.'s 4th.	1. P. to K.'s 4th.
2. P. to K. B.'s 4th.	2. P. takes P.
3. K. B. to Q. B.'s 4th.	3. Q. to R.'s 5th (ch.)
4. K. to B.'s sq.	4. P. to K. Kt.'s 4th.
5. Q. Kt. to B.'s 3rd.	5. B. to K. Kt.'s 2nd.
6. P. to Q.'s 4th.	6. Kt. to K.'s 2nd.
7. P. to K. Kt.'s 3rd. (*a*)	7. P. takes P.
8. K. to Kt.'s 2nd. (*b*)	8. Q. to R.'s 3rd.
9. P. takes P.	9. Q. to K. Kt.'s 3rd.
10. Kt. to K. B.'s 3rd.	10. P. to K. R.'s 3rd.
11. P. to Q.'s Kt.'s 3rd. (*c*)	11. P. to Q.'s 3rd.
12. P. to K.'s 5th.	12. Q. B. to K. Kt.'s 5th.
13. B. to Q.'s 3d.	13. P. to K. B.'s 4th.
14. Kt. to Q. Kt.'s 5th.	14. K. to Q.'s sq.
15. B. to Q. R.'s 3rd.	15. Kt. to Q.'s 4th.
16. Q. to Q.'s 2nd.	16. Q. B. takes Kt. (ch.)
17. K. takes B.	17. P. takes P.
18. P. takes P.	18. Q. Kt. to Q.'s 2nd.
19. Q. R. to K.'s sq.	19. P. to Q. R.'s 3rd.
20. Kt. to Q.'s 4th.	20. P. to Q. B.'s 4th.
21. B. takes K. B.'s P.	21. K. R. to K. B.'s sq.
22. K. to K. Kt.'s 4th. (*d*)	22. K. R. takes B.
23. Kt. takes R.	23. Q. to K.'s 3rd.
24. B. takes Q. B. P.	24. K. to Q. B.'s sq.
25. Q. takes Kt.	25. Q. takes Q.
26. Kt. to K.'s 7th (ch.)	26. K. to Q.'s sq

27. Kt. takes Q.
28. P. to K.'s 6th.
29. K. R. to K. B.'s sq.

27. Kt. takes B.
28. K. to K.'s sq.

And black resigns.

(*a*) A strong move, not found in "the books."
(*b*) Bold but safe.   (*c*) A most subtle move.   (*d*) Masterly play.

NOTE.—The above beautiful specimen of the Bishop's Gambit is transla
ted from the Berlin Chess Magazine by Mr. Daniel S. Roberts, of the Brook
lyn Chess-club, one of the finest players in the United States.

EVANS'S GAMBIT.

WHITE. Herr Anderssen.   BLACK. M. Dufresne.

1. P. to K.'s 4th.   1. P. to K.'s 4th.
2. Kt. to K. B.'s 3rd.   2. Kt. to Q. B's 3rd.
3. B. to Q. B.'s 4th.   3. B. to Q. B.'s 4th.
4. P. to Q. Kt.'s 4th.   4. B. takes Kt.'s P.
5. P. to Q. B.'s 3rd.   5. B. to. R.'s 4th.
6. P. to Q.'s 4th.   6. P. takes P.
7. Castles.   7. P. to Q.'s 6th.
8. Q. to Q. Kt.'s 3rd.   8. Q. to B.'s 3rd.
9. R. to K.'s sq.   9. B. to Q. Kt.'s 3rd.
10. P. to K.'s 5th.   10. Q. to Kt.'s 3rd.
11. Q. to Q.'s sq.   11. Kt. to R.'s 3rd.
12. B. takes Q.'s P.   12. Q. to R's 4th.
13. P. to K. R.'s 3rd.   13. Kt. to K.'s 2nd.
14. Kt. to Q.'s 2nd.   14. P. to Q.'s 4th.
15. P. takes P. (*en passant*).   15. P. takes P.
16. Kt. to Q. B.'s 4th.   16. B. to Q. B.'s 4th.
17. B. to K. Kt.'s 5th.   17. P. to B.'s 3rd.
18. Kt. takes P. (ch.)   18. B. takes Kt.
19. B. to Kt.'s 5th (ch.)   19. K. to B.'s sq.
20. Q. takes B.   20. K. Kt. to B.'s 4th.
21. Q. to Q.'s 8th (ch.)   21. K. to B.'s 2nd.
22. R. takes Kt. (ch.)   22. Kt. takes R.
23. Kt. to K.'s 5th (ch.)   Black resigns.

SICILIAN OPENING.

WHITE. Herr Lowenthal.   BLACK. Rev. T. Gordon

1. P. to K.'s 4th.   1. P. to Q. B.'s 4th.
2. K. Kt. to K. B.'s 3rd.   2. P. to K.'s 3rd.
3. Q. Kt. to Q. B.'s 3rd.   3. Q. Kt. to B.'s 3rd.
4. K. B. to Q. Kt.'s 5th.   4. Q. Kt. to K.'s 2nd.
5. P. to K.'s 5th. (*a*)   5. Q. Kt. to K. Kt.'s 3rd.
6. P. to Q.'s 4th.   6. P. to Q. R.'s 3rd.
7. K. B. to K.'s 2nd.   7. Q. to Q B.'s 2nd.
8. Q. B. to K.'s 3rd.   8. P. to Q.'s 4th. (*b*)
9. P. takes P. (in passing).   9. B. takes P.
10. Q. Kt. to K.'s 4th.   10. P. takes P.
11. B. takes P.   11. B. to K. B.'s sq. (*c*)
12. Castles.   12. K. Kt. to K. R.'s 3rd.
13. Q. B. to Q. B.'s 3rd.   13. K. Kt. to K. B.'s 4th.
14. Q. to Q.'s 2nd.   14. P. to K. B.'s 3rd.
15. Q. R. to Q.'s sq.   15. K. B. to K.'s 2nd.
16. P. to K. R.'s 3rd.   16. Castles.
17. P. to K. Kt.'s 4th   17. K. Kt. to R.'s 5th.
18. K. Kt. takes Kt.   18. Kt. takes Kt.

19. Kt. to K. Kt.'s 3rd.	19. P. to Q. Kt.'s 4th. (*d*)
20. P. to K. B.'s 4th.	20. Q. to Q. B.'s 3rd.
21. R. to K. B.'s 2nd.	21. K. R. to Q.'s sq.
22. Q. to K.'s 3rd.	22. Q. B. to Q. Kt.'s 2nd.
23. K. to R.'s 2nd.	23. R. takes R.
24. B. takes R.	24. R. to Q.'s sq.
25. R. to Q.'s 2nd.	25. R. takes R. (ch.)
26. Q. takes R.	26. B. to Q.'s 3rd.
27. Kt. to K. R.'s 5th.	27. Kt. to K. Kt.'s 3rd.
28. K. to Kt.'s 3rd.	28. P. to K.'s 4th.
29. P. to K. B.'s 5th.	29. Kt. to K. B.'s 5th.
30. Q. to K. B.'s 2nd.	30. Q. to K. R.'s 8th.
31. Kt. takes Kt.	31. P. takes Kt. (ch.)
32. K. to R.'s 5th.	32. B. to K. Kt.'s 7th.

And white resigns.

(*a*) The opening is very well played on the part of white, and for some time is decidedly in his favor.

(*b*) P. to K. B.'s 3rd would perhaps have been better play.

(*c*) This was compulsory, and it very much retarded the development of black's game. That after being obliged to retreat thus, he should have freed his men and fairly forced his adversary to act on the defensive, is highly creditable to his skill and persevering courage.

(*d*) P. to K. B.'s 4th would also have been a good move.

SCOTCH GAMBIT.

A dashing skirmish between Count Vitzhum and Mr. Falkbeer.

BLACK. Count Vitzhum.	WHITE. Mr. Falkbeer.
1. P. to K.'s 4th.	1. P. to K.'s 4th.
2. K. Kt. to K. B.'s 3rd.	2. Q. Kt. to Q. B.'s 3rd.
3. P. to Q.'s 4th.	3. P. takes P.
4. K. B. to Q. B.'s 4th.	4. K. B. to Q. B.'s 4th.
5. K. Kt. to Kt.'s 5th.	5. K. Kt. to K. R.'s 3rd.
6. Q. to K. R.'s 5th.	6. Q. to K.'s 2nd.
7. K. Kt. to K. B.'s 3rd.	7. K. B. checks.
8. P. to Q. B.'s 3rd.	8. P. takes P.
9. Castles.	9. P. to Q.'s 3rd.
10. P. takes P.	10. K. B. to Q. B.'s 4th.
11. Q. B. to K. Kt.'s 5th.	11. Q. B. to K. Kt.'s 5th.
12. Q. to K. R.'s 4th.	12. Q. to Q.'s 2nd.
13. Q. B. takes Kt.	13. P. takes B.
14. Q. Kt. to Q.'s 2nd.	14. Q. B. takes K. Kt.
15. Kt. takes B.	15. Q. to K.'s 2nd.
16. Q. takes P.	16. Castles on Q.'s side.
17. B. to Q.'s 5th.	17. Kt. to K.'s 4th.
18. Kt. takes Kt.	18. Q. takes Kt.
19. Q. R. to Q. Kt.'s sq.	19. B. to Q. Kt.'s 3rd.
20. Q. to K. R.'s 3rd (ch.)	20. K. to Kt.'s sq.
21. P. to Q. R.'s 4th.	21. P. to Q. R.'s 4th.
22. Q. R. to Q. Kt.'s 5th.	22. Q. to K. B.'s 3rd.
23. K. to R.'s sq.	23. Q. R. to K. Kt.'s sq. (*a*)
24. R. takes B.	

And white cannot save the game (*b*).

(*a*) A fatal oversight.

(*b*) Because, on his taking the rook, there follows Q. to Q.'s 7th, &c.

FRENCH OPENING.

Game between Messrs. Petroff and Szymanski, played at Warsaw.

WHITE. Mr. Petroff.   BLACK. Mr. Szymanski.

1. P. to K.'s 4th.	1. P. to K.'s 3rd.
2. P. to Q.'s 4th.	2. P. to Q.'s 4th.
3. P. takes P.	3. P. takes P.
4. P. to Q. B.'s 4th.	4. B. to Q. Kt.'s 5th (ch.)
5. Kt. to Q. B.'s 3rd.	5. Kt. to K.'s 2nd.
6. Kt. to K. B.'s 3rd.	6. B. to K. Kt.'s 5th.
7. B. to K.'s 2nd.	7. P. takes P. (a)
8. Castles.	8. B. takes K. Kt.
9. B. takes B.	9. P. to Q. B.'s 3rd.
10. Q. to K.'s 2nd.	10. Q. takes Q. P. (b)
11. R. to Q.'s sq.	11. Q. to K. B.'s 3rd.
12. Kt. to K.'s 4th. (c)	12. Q. to K.'s 3rd.
13. P. to Q. R.'s 3rd.	13. B. to Q. R.'s 4th.
14. B. to K. Kt.'s 4th. (d)	14. Q. to K. Kt.'s 3rd.
15. B. to K. B.'s 5th. (e)	15. Kt. takes B.

And white mates in two moves.

(a) Better to have castled than aim at this petty capture.
(b) Again black would have acted more wisely in castling. This second prize will prove a fatal acquisition.
(c) The attack now obtained is capitally carried out.
(d) This wins the queen, play as black may. For if—

	14. P. to K. B.'s 4th.
15. Kt. to Q.'s 6th (ch.)	15. K. to Q.'s 2nd (best).
16. Kt. takes Q. Kt. P. (dis. ch.)	16. Kt. to Q.'s 4th.
17. Kt. to Q. B.'s 5th (ch.), &c., &c.	

(e) Very elegant and decisive.

MUZIO GAMBIT.

Between Mr. Szen, of Hungary, and V. H. der Laza, of the Berlin Chess-club.

WHITE. V. H. der Laza.   BLACK. Mr. Szen.

1. P. to K.'s 4th.	1. P. to K.'s 4th.
2. P. to K. B.'s 4th.	2. P. takes P.
3. K. Kt. to B.'s 3rd.	3. P. to Kt.'s 4th.
4. B. to Q. B.'s 4th.	4. P. to K. Kt.'s 5th.
5. Castles.	5. P. takes Kt.
6. Q. takes P.	6. Q. to K. B.'s 3rd.
7. P. to K.'s 5th.	7. Q. takes K. P.
8. P. to Q.'s 3rd.	8. K. B. to K. R.'s 3rd.
9. Kt. to Q. B.'s 3rd.	9. K. Kt. to K.'s 2nd.
10. Q. B. to Q.'s 2nd.	10. Castles. (a)
11. Q. R. to K.'s sq.	11. Q. to Q. B.'s 4th (ch.)
12. K. to R.'s sq.	12. P. to Q. B.'s 3rd.
13. Kt. to K.'s 4th.	13. Q. to K. B.'s 4th.
14. Q. B. to his 3rd.	14. B. to K. Kt.'s 2nd.
15. Kt. to Q.'s 6th.	15. Q. to K. Kt.'s 4th.
16. R. takes Kt. (b)	16. B. takes Q. B. (c)
17. R. takes K. B. P.	17. R. takes R.
18. B. takes R. (ch.)	18. K. to Kt.'s 2nd.
19. P. takes B.	19. Kt. to Q. R.'s 3rd.

20. Q. takes K. B. P.	20. Q. takes Q.
21. R. takes Q.	21. Kt. to Q. B.'s 2nd.
22. B. to Q. Kt.'s 3rd.	22. Kt. to Q.'s 4th.
23. B. takes Kt	23. P. takes B.
24. R. to B.'s 7th (ch.)	24. K. to Kt.'s sq.
25. R. to K.'s 7th.	25. P. to Q. Kt.'s 3rd.
26. R. to K.'s 8th (ch.)	26. K. to Kt.'s 2nd.
27. R. takes B.	

And wins.

(*a*) Not considered so strong a move as 10. P. to Q. B.'s 3rd.

(*b*) Well played.

(*c*) Had he taken R. with Q., white would have won a piece by at once playing Kt. to K. B.'s 5th.

KING'S BISHOP'S OPENING.

Played by correspondence, between the Norfolk and New York Chess-clubs.

NORFOLK.	NEW YORK.
1. K. P. 2.	1. K. P. 2.
2. K. B. to Q. B.'s 4th.	2. K. B. to Q. B.'s 4th.
3. Q. B. P. 1.	3. Q. to K. Kt.'s 4th.
4. Q. to K. B.'s 3rd.	4. Q. to K. Kt.'s 3rd.
5. K. Kt. to K.'s 2nd.	5. Q. P. 1.
6. Q. P. 2.	6. K. B. to Q. Kt.'s 3rd.
7. Castles.	7. K. Kt. to B.'s 3rd.
8. P. takes P.	8. P. takes P.
9. Kt. to K. Kt.'s 3rd.	9. Q. B. to K. Kt.'s 5th.
10. Q. to Q.'s 3rd.	10. Q. Kt. to Q.'s 2nd.
11. Q. Kt. P. 2.	11. K. Kt. to R.'s 4th.
12. Q. B. to K.'s 3rd.	12. Castles (Q. R.)
13. Kt. takes Kt.	13. B. takes Kt.
14. Kt. to Q.'s 2nd.	14. Kt. to K. B.'s 3rd.
15. Q. to Q. B.'s 2nd.	15. R. takes Kt.
16. Q. takes R.	16. Kt. takes P.
17. Q. to Q. B.	17. B. to K. B.'s 6th.
18. K. Kt. P. 1.	18. K. R. P. 2.
19. K. B. to Q.'s 5th.	19. K. R. P. 1.
20. B. takes Kt.	20. Q. takes B.
21. B. takes B.	21. Q. to K. Kt.'s 5th.
22. Q. to K.'s 3rd.	22. R. P. takes B.
23. K. R. to Q. Kt.	23. K. P. 1.
24. Q. to K.	24. K. B. P. 2.
25. R. to Kt.'s 2nd.	25. K. B. P. 1.
26. Q. R. to Q. Kt.	

New York Checkmates in four moves.

So handsome a termination to a game played by *correspondence* is indeed rare; the position, as it now stands, is a very pretty problem—solution as follows:

	26. Q. to R.'s 6th.
27. Q. to K. B.	27. Q. takes R. P. (ch.)
28. K. takes Q.	28. R. P. takes P. (ch.)
29. K. to Kt.	29. R. checkmates.

NOTE.—The present officers (1857) of the New York Chess-club are Col. O. D. Mead, President, and F. Perrin, Esq., Secretary. The club numbers some seventy members. Its leading players are Messrs. Stanley, Thompson. Mead, Perrin, Marache, Lichtenhein, Montgomery, Loyd, Raphael, Fuller, Gallatin, Anderson, Bernier, Jullien, and King; and embraces some very promising younger players, among whom are Messrs. Fisk, Quimby, Hazeltine, Miller, and the younger Loyd.

KING'S BISHOP'S OPENING.

Played at New Orleans, between Messrs. Rousseau and Stanley, being the first game occurring in a match between those gentlemen. With notes by M. St. Amant, the editor of the *Palaméde*, Paris.

WHITE. Stanley.	BLACK. Rousseau.
1. K. P. 2.	1. K. P. 2.
2. K. B. to Q. B.'s 4th.	2. K. Kt. to B.'s 3rd. (a)
3. Q. Kt. to B.'s 3rd.	3. K. B. to Q. B.'s 4th.
4. K. Kt. to B.'s 3rd.	4. Q. P. 1.
5. K. R. P. 1.	5. Castles.
6. Q. P. 1.	6. Q. B. to K.'s 3rd.
7. K. B. to Kt.'s 3rd. (b)	7. Q. Kt. to B.'s 3rd.
8. Q. Kt. to K.'s 2nd. (c)	8. Q. to K.'s 2nd.
9. Q. Kt. to K. Kt.'s 3rd. (d)	9. Q. Kt. to Q.'s 5th. (e)
10. Kt. takes Kt.	10. B. takes Kt.
11. Q. B. P. 1.	11. B. to Kt.'s 3rd. (f)
12. Castles.	12. Q. P. 1. (g)
13. Q. B. to K. Kt.'s 5th.	13. Q. B. P. 1.
14. Kt. to K. R.'s 5th.	14. P. takes P.
15. P. takes P.	15. B. takes B.
16. Q. to K. B.'s 3rd. (h)	16. Q. B. to its 5th.
17. B. takes Kt.	17. Q. to K.'s 3rd. (i)
18. Kt. takes Kt. P.	18. Q. B. to K.'s 7th.
19. Kt. takes Q.	19. B. takes Q.
20. Kt. takes R. (j)	

Black resigns.

(a) A commendable move, giving more power to the defence than bringing out K. B. to Q. B.'s 4th.

(b) This move, which looks like a lost one, is the correct reply. We now prefer white's game, notwithstanding the retreat of bishop.

(c) This retreat of knight has no appearance of brilliancy about it, but " denotes a player well versed in the science of counter-marches.

(d) Black having castled, white brings up force to act powerfully in the proper quarter.

(e) A weak move. Black loses a *time* (*un temps*) by it, and in an opening, even at the eleventh move, a *time* is most precious.

(f) The effect of the *time lost* we have just mentioned.

(g) Black's position being still one of some constraint, he should have avoided this abrupt attack, and more especially in the centre. K. R. P. 1 would have been more solid play, and would have avoided the very rapid subsequent decline, in a game still so nearly equal.

(h) Masterly play. If the white, instead of playing queen to this square, had recaptured adverse bishop, the game would have remained a long time undecided. Here, on the contrary, every stroke tells. An instructive example, admitting of frequent appreciation. It must be presumed, that when black captured bishop, he overlooked *the possibility* of white's not recapturing immediately.

(i) The capture of bishop with pawn would entail the sacrifice of queen to avoid checkmate. Black's game has assumed a deplorable aspect, all resulting from not having pushed K. R. P. 1 at the proper time, thus preventing his adversary planting a bishop at knight's 5th—a move generally productive of much embarrassment.

(*j*) No resource left. A short game, with a most rapid falling off, after black's injudicious attack at the thirteenth move.

THE KNIGHT'S GAME OF RUY LOPEZ.

BLACK. Mr. Greenaway.	WHITE. Herr Anderssen.
1. K. P. 2.	1. K. P. 2.
2. K. Kt. to B.'s 3rd.	2. Q. Kt. to B.'s 3rd.
3. K. B. to Q. B.'s 4th.	3. K. B. to B.'s 4th.
4. Q. Kt. P. 2.	4. B. takes P.
5. Q. B. P. 1.	5. B. to R.'s 4th.
6. Castles. (*a*)	6. K. Kt. to B.'s 3rd.
7. Q. P. 2.	7. Castles.
8. Q. to Q. B.'s 2nd.	8. Q. to K.'s 2nd.
9. Q. Kt. to Q.'s 2nd.	9. P. takes P.
10. P. takes P.	10. B. takes Kt.
11. B. takes B.	11. Q. takes P.
12. K. B. to Q.'s 3rd.	12. Q. to K. Kt.'s 5th.
13. K. B. to B.'s 5th.	13. Kt. takes P.
14. Kt. takes Kt.	14. Q. takes Kt.
15. B. to Q. B.'s 3rd.	15. Q. to Q. Kt.'s 3rd. (*b*)
16. B. takes Kt.	16. Q. takes B.
17. B. takes R. P. (ch.)	17. K. to R.'s sq.
18. B. to K.'s 4th.	18. Q. B. P. 1.
19. K. B. P. 2.	19. Q. P. 2.
20. B. to Q.'s 3rd.	20. Q. Kt. P. 1. (*c*)
21. Q. R. to K.'s sq.	21. Q. B. P. 1.
22. Q. to K.'s 2nd.	22. K. to Kt.'s sq.
23. K. B. P. 1.	23. B. to Q. Kt.'s 2nd.
24. K. R. to B.'s 3rd.	24. Q. P. 1.
25. K. R. to R.'s 3rd.	25. Q. to Q. B.'s 3rd. (*d*)
26. K. B. P. 1. (*e*)	26. K. Kt. P. 1.
27. B. to K.'s 4th.	27. Q. takes B.
28. Q. takes Q.	28. B. takes Q.
29. R. takes B.	29. K. R. to K.'s sq. (*f*)
30. Q. R. to K. R.'s 4th.	White resigned.

(*a*) Q. P. 2 at once is much more attacking.

(*b*) Q. to Q. B.'s 4th, with a view to exchange queens, would, we think, have been better.

(*c*) K. Kt. P. 1, followed by B. to K. B.'s 4th, would have relieved him greatly from his embarrassed position.

(*d*) In order to play Q. R. to K.'s square, which he clearly could not have done before.

(*e*) Beautiful move; if white plays K. R. to K.'s square, black mates in four moves by sacrificing his K. R.; if Q. takes P., black mates in five moves, as follows:

26. K. B. P. 1.	26. Q. takes B. P.
27. B. to R.'s 7th (ch.)	27. K. to R.'s sq.
28. B. to K. Kt.'s 6th (ch.)	28. K. to Kt.'s sq.
29. R. to K. R.'s 8th (ch)	29. K. takes R.
30. Q. to R 's 5th (ch.)	30. K. to Kt.'s sq.
31. Q. to R.'s 7th. Mate.	

(*f*) He has nothing better; if he play K. Kt. P. 1, black plays Q. R. to Kt.'s 4th, mating in two moves.

ALGAIER GAMBIT.

Between MM. Kieseritzky and Calvi.

WHITE. M. Kieseritzky.	BLACK. M. Calvi.
1. P. to K.'s 4th.	1. P. to K.'s 4th.
2. P. to K. B.'s 4th.	2. P. takes P.
3. K. Kt. to B.'s 3rd.	3. P. to K. Kt.'s 4th.
4. P. to K. R.'s 4th.	4. P. to K. Kt.'s 5th.
5. Kt. to K.'s 5th.	5. P. to K. R.'s 4th.
6. K. B. to Q. B.'s 4th.	6. R. to K. R.'s 2nd
7. P. to Q.'s 4th.	7. P. to Q.'s 3rd.
8. Kt. to Q.'s 3rd.	8. P. to K. B.'s 6th.
9. P. takes P.	9. P. to Q. B.'s 3rd.
10. K. Kt. to B.'s 4th.	10. K. Kt. to K.'s 2nd.
11. Q. Kt. to B.'s 3rd.	11. Q. Kt. to Q.'s 2nd.
12. K. to B.'s 2nd.	12. R. to K. R.'s sq.
13. Q. to her 3rd.	13. K. B. to Kt.'s 2nd.
14. Q. B. to Q.'s 2nd.	14. K. to B.'s sq.
15. Q. R. to K.'s sq.	15. Q. to her Kt.'s 3rd.
16. Q. B. to K.'s 3rd.	16. Q. to Q. B.'s 2nd.
17. K. B. to K.'s 6th.	17. P. to Q. Kt.'s 4th.
18. P. to Q. Kt.'s 4th.	18. Q. Kt. to his 3rd.
19. K. B. to Q. Kt.'s 3rd.	19. P. to Q. R.'s 4th.
20. P. to Q. R.'s 3rd.	20. P. to Q. R.'s 5th.
21. B. to Q. R.'s 2nd.	21. Q. B. to Kt.'s 2nd.
22. P. to K.'s 5th.	22. P. to Q.'s 4th.
23. P. to K.'s 6th.	23. Q. B. to his sq.
24. Q. B. to his sq.	24. Q. to her 3rd.
25. P. takes P.	25. K. takes P.
26. Q. Kt. to K.'s 4th.	26. Q. to her B.'s 2nd.
27. Q. Kt. to K. Kt.'s 5th (ch.)	27. K. to Kt.'s sq.
28. R. takes Kt.	28. Q. takes R.
29. R. to K.'s sq.	29. Q. to K. B.'s 3rd.
30. R. to K.'s 8th (ch.)	30. B. to K. B.'s sq.
31. K. Kt. to Kt.'s 6th.	31. Q. B. to K. B.'s 4th.
32. Q. takes B. (a)	32. Q. takes Q.
33. Kt. to K.'s 7th (ch.)	33. K. to Kt.'s 2nd.
34. Kt. takes Q. (ch.)	34. K. to B.'s 3rd.
35. R. to K.'s 6th (ch.)	35. K. takes Kt.
36. B. to Q. Kt.'s sq.	

And mates next move.

(*a*) The termination of this game is very beautifully played by M Kieseritzky.

THE LOPEZ GAMBIT.

Between Messrs. De la Bourdonnais and McDonnell.

WHITE. M. De la B.	BLACK. Mr. McD.
1. P. to K.'s 4th.	1. P. to K.'s 4th.
2. K. B. to Q. B.'s 4th.	2. K. B. to Q. B.'s 4th.
3. Q. to K.'s 2nd.	3. K. Kt. to B.'s 3rd.
4. P. to Q.'s 3rd.	4. Q. Kt. to B.'s 3rd.
5. P. to Q. B.'s 3rd.	5. Q. Kt. to K.'s 2nd.
6. P. to K. B.'s 4th..	6. P. takes P. (a)
7. P. to Q.'s 4th.	7. K. B. to Kt.'s 3rd.
8. Q. B. takes P.	8. P. to Q.'s 3rd.

9. K. B. to Q.'s 3rd.
0. Q. B. to K.'s 3rd.
1. P. to K. R.'s 3rd.
12. Q. Kt. to Q.'s 2nd.
13. Castles on Q.'s side
14. K. to Kt.'s sq.
15. P. takes P.
16. K. Kt. to B.'s 3rd.
17. P. to K. Kt.'s 4th.
18. Q. R. to K. Kt.'s sq.
19. P. to K. Kt.'s 5th.
20. R. takes P.
21. P. to Q. Kt.'s 3rd.
22. Q. R. to K. Kt.'s 4th.
23. P. to K. R.'s 4th.
24. Kt. takes B.
25. P. to K. R.'s 5th.
26. R. takes R.
27. Q. to K. B.'s 3rd.
28. P. to Q.'s 5th.
29. K. R. to K. Kt.'s sq. (b)
30. K. to R.'s sq.
31. R. takes K. Kt. P. (ch.)
32. Q. to K. Kt.'s 3rd.
33. K. R. P. takes B.
34. R. takes Q.
35. Q. takes R.
36. R. to R.'s 7th (ch.)
37. P. takes K. B. P. (ch.)
38. P. 1, becoming a queen.

9. Q. Kt. to K. Kt.'s 3rd.
10. Castles.
11. K. R. to K.'s sq.
12. Q. to K.'s 2nd.
13. P. to Q. B.'s 4th.
14. P. takes P.
15. P. to Q. R.'s 4th.
16. Q. B. to Q.'s 2nd.
17. P. to K. R.'s 3rd.
18. P. to Q. R.'s 5th.
19. P. takes P.
20. P. to Q. R.'s 6th.
21. Q. B. to his 3rd.
22. K. B. to Q. R.'s 4th.
23. B. takes Q. Kt.
24. Q. R. to his 4th.
25. R. takes B.
26. Kt. to K. B.'s 5th.
27. Kt. takes B.
28. Kt. takes Q. P.
29. Kt. to B.'s 6th (ch.)
30. B. takes K. P.
31. K. to R.'s sq.
32. B. to K. Kt.'s 3rd.
33. Q. to K.'s 8th (ch.)
34. R. takes R. (ch.)
35. Kt. takes Q.
36. K. to Kt.'s sq.
37. K. takes R.
38. Kt. mates.

(a) In this opening it is not advisable for the second player to take the gambit pawn with his king's pawn.
(b) This portion of the game is full of interest and instruction, and is remarkably well played.

QUEEN'S GAMBIT.

Between Messrs. Harrwitz and Lowenthal.

BLACK. **Mr. Harrwitz.**

1. Q. P. 2.
2. Q. B. P. 2.
3. K. P. 2.
4. Q. P. 1.
5. Q. Kt. to B.'s 3rd.
6. Q. B. to K. Kt.'s 5th.
7. K. B. takes P.
8. K. Kt. to B.'s 3rd.
9. B. takes Kt.
10. Q. to K.'s 2nd. (b)
11. P. takes P.
12. K. B. to Q.'s 3rd.
13. Q. Kt. to K.'s 4th.
14. Kt. takes Kt.
15. Castles K. R.
16. B. to K.'s 4th.
17. Q. R. to B.'s sq.
18. K. R. P. 1.
19. P. takes B.

WHITE. **Mr. Lowenthal.**

1. Q. P. 2.
2. P. takes P.
3. K. P. 2.
4. K. B. P. 2.
5. K. Kt. to B.'s 3rd.
6. K. B. to Q.'s 3rd. (a)
7. Castles.
8. K. R. P. 1.
9. Q. takes B.
10. Q. Kt. to Q.'s 2nd.
11. Q. takes P.
12. Q. to K. R.'s 4th. (c)
13. Kt. to Q. B.'s 4th.
14. B. takes Kt.
15. Q. B. to K. Kt.'s 5th.
16. R. to B.'s 5th.
17. K. B. to Q.'s 3rd.
18. Q. R. to K. B.'s sq. (d)
19. Q. takes P.

20. K. R. to K.'s sq.	20. B. to Q. Kt.'s 5th. (*e*)
21. Kt. to R.'s 2. (*f*)	21. Q. to Kt.'s 4th.
22. K. R. to B.'s sq. (*g*)	22. R. takes P.
23. R. takes R.	23. Q. takes R. (ch.)
24. R. to B.'s sq.	24. R. takes R. (ch.)
25. Kt. takes R.	25. B. to B.'s 4th (ch.)
26. K. to R.'s 2nd.	26. B. to Q.'s 5th.
27. Q. Kt. P. 1.	27. Q. to K. Kt.'s 4th.
28. K. Kt. P. 1.	28. K. to B.'s 2nd.
29. Q. to B.'s 3rd (ch.)	29. K. to K.'s 2nd.
30. Q. to B.'s 5th.	30. Q. takes Q.
31. B. takes Q.	31. Q. B. P. 1.
32. P. takes P.	32. P. takes P.
33. K. to R.'s 3rd.	33. K. Kt. P. 2.
34. Kt. to Q.'s 2nd.	34. K. R. P. 1.
35. B. to K. Kt.'s 6th.	35. K. R. P. 1.
36. P. takes P.	36. P. takes P.
37. K. takes P.	37. K. to Q.'s 3rd.
38. K. to Kt.'s 4th. (*h*)	38. K. to B.'s 4th.
39. K. to B.'s 5th.	39. K. to Kt.'s 5th.
40. Kt. to Q. B.'s 4th.	40. Q. B. P. 1.
41. B. to B.'s 7th.	41. Q. R. P. 2.
42. Kt. to Q. Kt.'s 6th.	42. K. to R.'s 6th.
43. B. to Q. B.'s 4th.	43. B. to Q. B.'s 6th. (*i*)
44. Kt. to Q.'s 5th.	44. B. to Q. Kt.'s 5th.
45. Kt. takes B.	45. B. P. takes Kt.
46. B. to Q. Kt.'s 5th (*j*)	

And white resigned.   Duration, seven hours.

(*a*) We should certainly have preferred playing K. B. to Q. B.'s 4th.

(*b*) Had he castled, white might have obtained an almost irresistible attack by advancing his pawns on king's side.

(*c*) If Q. to Kt.'s 5th, black replies with Q. to K.'s 4th, and if then Q. takes Kt. P., white would lose the game in a few moves, as the following variation shows. Suppose :

	12. Q. to K. Kt.'s 5th.
13. Q. to K.'s 4th.	13. Q. takes Kt. P.
14. K. R. to Kt.'s sq.	14. Q. takes Kt.

And black checkmates in three moves.

(*d*) A miscalculation, and yet white took twenty minutes over this move.

(*e*) White consumed twenty-six minutes over this move.

(*f*) We believe he might have taken K. P. with safety.

(*g*) Black gives up another pawn in order to exchange pieces

(*h*) Kt. to K.'s 4th (ch.), before moving K., would have been safer; but the best was to play Q. R. P. 2 and B. to K. B.'s 7th.

(*i*) Had he taken R.'s P. with K., Kt.'s P. would have become a Q.

(*j*) The only winning move.

QUEEN'S GAMBIT DECLINED.

BLACK. Mr. Harrwitz.	WHITE. Mr. Lowenthal.
1. Q. P. 2.	1. Q. P. 2.
2. Q. B. P. 2.	2. K. P. 1.
3. Q. Kt. to B.'s 3rd.	3. K. Kt. to B.'s 3rd.
4. Q. B. to K. B.'s 4th.	4. K. B. to Q. Kt.'s 5th.
5. K. P. 1.	5. P. takes P.
6. K. B. takes P.	6. Kt. to Q.'s 4th.
7. K. Kt. to K.'s 2nd.	7. B. takes Kt. (ch.)
8. P. takes B.	8. Q. Kt. to B.'s 3rd.

9. Castles.	9. Kt. takes B.
10. Kt. takes Kt.	10. K. P. 1.
11. Kt. to R.'s 5th.	11. Castles. (a)
12. K. B. P. 2.	12. P. takes Q. P.
13. B. P. takes P.	13. Q. to K.'s 2nd.
14. Q. to K. B.'s 3rd.	14. K. Kt. P. 1.
15. Kt. to Kt.'s 3rd.	15. Q. to K. R.'s 5th.
16. Kt. to K.'s 4th.	16. K. to Kt.'s 2nd. (b)
17. K. Kt. P. 1.	17. Q. to K.'s 2nd.
18. Q. P. 1. (c)	18. Kt. to R.'s 4th.
19. B. to K.'s 2nd. (d)	19. B. to B.'s 4th. (e)
20. Kt. to B.'s 2nd.	20. K. R. to K.'s sq.
21. K. P. 1.	21. K. B. P. 1. (f)
22. Q. to Q. B.'s 3rd.	22. Q. Kt. P. 1.
23. K. B. to B.'s 3rd.	23. B. to Q.'s 2nd.
24. K. R. to K.'s sq.	24. Q. R. to Q. B.'s sq.
25. K. P. 1.	25. Kt. to Kt.'s 2nd.
26. Q. P. 1.	26. Kt. takes P.
27. P. takes Kt.	27. Q. takes P.
28. Q. R. to Q.'s sq.	28. R. takes R. (ch.)
29. Q. takes R.	29. Q. to K.'s 3rd.
30. Q. to Q. B.'s 3rd.	30. Q. to K.'s 2nd.
31. B. to Q. Kt.'s 7th.	31. R. to K.'s sq.
32. Q. takes Q. B. P.	32. B. to R.'s 5th.
33. R. to Q. B.'s sq.	33. K. to B.'s sq.
34. Q. takes Q. (ch.)	34. R. takes Q.
35. R. to B.'s 8th (ch.)	35. K. to Kt.'s 2nd.
36. B. to Q.'s 5th.	36. K. R. P. 2.
37. Kt. to K.'s 4th.	37. B. to K.'s sq.
38. Kt. to Q.'s 6th.	38. B. to R.'s 5th.
39. K. B. P. 1.	39. R. to K.'s 8th (ch.)
40. K. to B.'s 2nd.	40. R. to Q.'s 8th.

And black announced mate in four moves. (g) Duration, three hours.

(a) White has already an inferior game.

(b) He would evidently have lost a piece had he played B. to K. Kt.'s 5th, as black would have taken off B. with Q., and then, if Q. took Q., have checked with Kt.

(c) This puts the adverse Kt. out of play.

(d) To Q.'s 3rd would have been sounder play; the move in the text was played in anticipation of white's playing as he did the following moves.

(e) R. to K.'s square first would have won a pawn.

(f) If he had taken P. with B., black would have checked with Q. at B.'s 3rd, winning the Kt.

(g) This announcement came like a thunderbolt upon white, who had to look a long time before he discovered the way it is done.

PETROFF'S DEFENCE.

Between Von H. der Laza and Major Jaenisch.

WHITE. V. H. der L.	BLACK. Maj. J.
1. P. to K.'s 4th.	1. P. to K.'s 4th.
2. K. Kt. to B.'s 3rd.	2. K. Kt. to B.'s 3rd.
3. Kt. takes K. P.	3. P. to Q.'s 3rd.
4. Kt. to K. B.'s 3rd.	4. Kt. takes K. P.
5. P. to Q.'s 3rd.	5. Kt. to K. B.'s 3rd.
6. P. to Q.'s 4th.	6. P. to Q.'s 4th.
7. P. to K. R.'s 3rd.	7. K. B. to Q.'s 3rd.
8. Q. B. to K.'s 3rd.	8. Castles.
9. K. B. to K.'s 2nd.	9. Q. to K.'s 2nd.

10. P. to Q. B.'s 3rd.	10. P. to Q. B.'s 4th.
11. Q. to her B.'s 2nd.	11. Q. Kt. to B.'s 3rd.
12. Q. Kt. to Q.'s 2nd.	12. Q. B. to K.'s 3rd.
13. Q. P. takes P.	13. K. B. takes P.
14. B. takes B.	14. Q. takes B.
15. Q. Kt. to his 3rd.	15. Q. to her Kt.'s 3rd.
16. Castles on K.'s side.	16. Q. R. to Q. B.'s sq.
17. Q. to her 2nd.	17. K. R. to Q.'s sq.
18. Q. R. to Q.'s sq.	18. P. to Q. R.'s 3rd.
19. K. R. to K.'s sq.	19. K. R. to Q.'s 2nd.
20. K. B. to Q.'s 3rd.	20. Q. R. to Q.'s sq.
21. Q. Kt. to Q.'s 4th.	21. Q. R. to K.'s sq.
22. K. R. to K.'s 2nd.	22. K. R. to K.'s 2nd.
23. Q. R. to K.'s sq.	23. P. to K. R.'s 3rd.
24. Q. to K. B.'s 4th.	24. Q. Kt. to Q.'s sq
25. B. to K. B.'s 5th.	25. Q. to her B.'s 4th.
26. K. Kt. to K.'s 5th.	26. B. takes B.
27. Q. Kt. takes B.	27. Kt. to K.'s 3rd.
28. Kt. takes R. (ch.)	28. R. takes Kt.
29. Q. to K. B.'s 5th.	29. P. to Q.'s 5th.
30. K. R. to Q. B.'s 2nd.	30. P. to Q.'s 6th.
31. Q. takes Q. P.	31. Q. Kt. to K. B.'s 5th.
32. Q. to her 4th.	32. Q. takes Q.
33. P. takes Q.	33. K. Kt. to Q.'s 4th.
34. P. to Q. R.'s 3rd.	34. P. to K. Kt.'s 4th.
35. Kt. to K. B.'s 3rd.	35. R. takes R. (ch.)
36. Kt. takes R.	36. K. to Kt.'s 2nd.
37. R. to Q. B.'s 5th.	37. P. to Q. Kt.'s 3rd.
38. R. to B.'s 6th.	38. Q. Kt. to K.'s 3rd.
39. R. to Q.'s 6th.	39. K. Kt. to K. B.'s 5th.
40. Kt. to Q. B.'s 2nd.	40. K. Kt. to Q.'s 6th.
41. R. takes Q. Kt. P.	

And black surrendered.

KING'S GAMBIT.

Between V. H. der Laza and Dr. Bledow.

WHITE. V. H. der L.	BLACK. Dr. Bledow.
1. P. to K.'s 4th.	1. P. to K.'s 4th.
2. P. to K. B.'s 4th.	2. P. takes P.
3. K. Kt. to B.'s 3rd.	3. P. to K. Kt.'s 4th.
4. K. B. to Q. B.'s 4th.	4. K. B. to Kt.'s 2nd.
5. P. to Q.'s 4th.	5. Q. to K.'s 2nd. (a)
6. Castles.	6. P. to K. R.'s 3rd.
7. Q. Kt. to B.'s 3rd.	7. P. to Q. B.'s 3rd.
8. P. to K.'s 5th.	8. Q. to her Kt.'s 5th.
9. Q. Kt. to K.'s 4th.	9. K. B. to his sq.
10. Q. to K.'s 2nd. (b)	10. P. to K. Kt.'s 5th.
11. Kt. to Q.'s 6th (ch.)	11. B. takes Kt.
12. P. takes B. (dis. ch.)	12. K. to Q.'s sq.
13. Kt. to K.'s 5th.	13. R. to R.'s 2nd.
14. P. to Q. B.'s 3rd.	14. P. to K. B.'s 6th.
15. Q. to K.'s 4th.	15. K. Kt. to B.'s 3rd.
16. Q. takes R.	16. Kt. takes Q.

And white gave checkmate in six moves.

(a) The proper move is—5. P. to Q.'s 3rd.
(b) This little game is excellently played by white.

KING'S GAMBIT.

Between V. H. der Laza and Mr. H., of Berlin.

WHITE. V. H. der L.	BLACK. Mr. H.
1. P. to K.'s 4th.	1. P. to K.'s 4th.
2. P. to K. B.'s 4th.	2. P. takes P.
3. K. Kt. to B.'s 3rd.	3. P. to K. Kt.'s 4th.
4. K. B. to Q. B.'s 4th.	4. B. to K. Kt.'s 2nd.
5. Castles.	5. P. to K. R.'s 3rd.
6. P. to Q.'s 4th.	6. P. to Q.'s 3rd.
7. P. to Q. B.'s 3rd.	7. P. to Q. B.'s 3rd.
8. Q. to her Kt.'s 3rd. (a)	8. Q. to K.'s 2nd.
9. P. to K. Kt.'s 3rd.	9. P. to K. Kt.'s 5th.
10. Q. B. takes P.	10. P. takes Kt.
11. R. takes P.	11. Q. B. to K.'s 3rd.
12. P. to Q.'s 5th.	12. Q. B. to K. Kt.'s 5th.
13. P. takes Q. B. P.	13. B. takes R.
14. P. takes Kt. P.	14. Q. takes K. P.
15. P. takes R. (becoming a Q.)	15. Q. takes Q.
16. B. takes K. B. P. (ch.)	16. K. to B.'s sq.
17. B. takes Kt.	17. R. takes B.
18. B. takes Q. P. (ch.)	18. K. to K.'s sq.

White mates in three moves.

(a) Having now your Q. P. protected, and an opening for your queen, you can advantageously advance the K. Kt. P., and sacrifice your Kt., as in the muzio gambit.

KING'S GAMBIT.

Between Mr. Popert and an eminent Polish player.

WHITE. Mr. Z.	BLACK. Mr. P.
1. P. to K.'s 4th.	1. P. to K.'s 4th.
2. P. to K. B.'s 4th.	2. P. takes P.
3. K. Kt. to B.'s 3rd.	3. P. to K. Kt.'s 4th.
4. B. to Q. B.'s 4th.	4. B. to Q. Kt.'s 2nd.
5. P. to Q.'s 4th.	5. P. to Q.'s 3rd.
6. Castles.	6. P. to K. R.'s 3rd.
7. P. to K. Kt.'s 3rd.	7. P. to K. Kt.'s 5th.
8. K. Kt. to R.'s 4th.	8. P. to K. B.'s 6th.
9. Q. B. to K.'s 3rd.	9. Q. Kt. to B.'s 3rd.
10. P. to Q. B.'s 3rd.	10. K. B. to B.'s 3rd.
11. K. Kt. to K. B.'s 5th.	11. Q. B. takes Kt.
12. P. takes B.	12. K. Kt. to K.'s 2nd.
13. Q. to her Kt.'s 3rd.	13. P. to Q.'s 4th.
14. K. B. to Q.'s 3rd.	14. Q. to her 2nd.
15. Q. to her B.'s 2nd.	15. P. to K. R.'s 4th.
16. Kt. to Q.'s 2nd.	16. P. to K. R.'s 5th.
17. Q. B. to K. B.'s 4th.	17. Castles on Q.'s side.
18. P. to Q. R.'s 4th.	18. P. takes K. Kt. P.
19. Q. B. takes K. Kt. P.	19. K. R. to his 4th.
20. P. to Q. Kt.'s 4th.	20. K. Kt. takes K. B. P.
21. B. takes Kt.	21. Q. takes B.
22. Q. to her Kt.'s 2nd.	22. B. to K. R.'s 5th.
23. B. takes B.	23. R. takes B.
24. P. to Q. R.'s 5th.	24. R. takes K. R. P.
25. K. takes R.	

Black mates in three moves.

KING'S GAMBIT DECLINED.

BLACK. M. Journoud.	WHITE. Capt. Kennedy.
1. K. P. 2.	1. K. P. 1.
2. K B. P. 2.	2. Q. P. 2.
8 P. takes P.	8. P. takes P.
4. K. Kt. to B.'s 3rd.	4. K. B. to Q.'s 3rd.
5. Q. P. 2.	5. K. Kt. to B.'s 3rd.
6. K. B. to Q.'s 3rd.	6. Castles.
7. Castles.	7. Kt. to K.'s 5th.
8. Q. Kt. to B.'s 3rd.	8. Kt. takes Kt.
9. P. takes Kt.	9. Q. B. to K. Kt.'s 5th.
10. P. to Q. B.'s 4th.	10. Q. B. P. 1.
11. P. takes P.	11. P. takes P.
12. Q. B. P. 1. (a)	12. Kt. to Q.'s 2nd.
13. Q. to Q. B.'s 2nd.	13. K. Kt. P. 1.
14. Kt. to K.'s 5th.	14. Q. B. to K.'s 3rd.
15. K. B. P. 1. (b)	15. Kt. takes Kt.
16. P. takes Kt.	16. K. B. to Q. B.'s 4th (ch.)
17. K. to R.'s sq.	17. P. takes P.
18. B. takes P.	18. Q. to K. R.'s 5th.
19. Q. B. to Q.'s 2nd.	19. B. takes B.
20. Q. takes B.	20. Q. to K.'s 5th. (c)
21. Q. takes Q.	21. P. takes Q.
22. Q. R. to K.'s sq.	22. K. R. to Q.'s sq.
23. B. to R.'s 6th.	23. K. P. 1.
24. K. R. to B.'s 3rd.	24. R. to Q.'s 7th.
25. R. to Kt.'s 3rd (ch.)	25. K. to B.'s sq.
26. B. to Kt.'s 7th (ch.)	26. K. to Kt.'s sq.
27. B. to K. B.'s 6th (ch)	27. K. to B.'s sq.
28. R. to Kt.'s 7th.	28. B. to K.'s 2nd. (d)
29. K. R. takes P.	29. B. takes B.
30. P. takes B.	30. K. to Kt.'s sq.
31. R. to Kt.'s 7th (ch.)	31. K. to B.'s sq.
32. K. R. P. 2.	32. K. P. 1.
33. K. to Kt.'s sq.	33. Q. R. to K.'s sq.
34. K. Kt. P. 2.	34. Q. R. to K.'s 3rd.
35. K. Kt. P. 1.	35. R. to K.'s 5th.
36. K. R. P. 1.	36. R. to K. R.'s 5th.
37. K. Kt. P. 1.	37. P. takes P.
38. P. takes P.	38. R. to Q.'s 8th.
39. R. to K. B.'s 7th (ch.)	39. K. to Kt.'s sq.
40. K. to B.'s 2nd.	40. R. to K. R.'s 7th (ch.)
41. K. to Kt.'s 3rd.	41. R. takes R.
42. R. takes P.	42. R. to Kt.'s 7th (ch.)
43. K. takes R.	43. R. to Kt.'s 8th (ch.)
44. K. to B.'s 3rd.	44. R. takes P.
45. K. takes P.	45. R. to K. Kt.'s 7th (ch.)
46. K. to Q.'s 3rd.	46. R. takes P.
47. K. to Q.'s 4th.	47. R. to Q. R.'s 3rd.
48. Q. B. P. 1.	48. R. takes P.
49. R. takes P. And wins.	

(a) Q. B. P. 2 would here have been stronger; it would have given black a passed pawn.

(b) Well played; this puts white still more on the defensive.

(c) White judiciously seeks an exchange of queens, even though it cost him a pawn, because he fears the joint attack from black's rook and bishop upon his king.

(d) His only move t` prevent fatal loss.

IRREGULAR OPENING.

In a match between Messrs. Thompson and Marache, both of the N. Y. Chess-club.

WHITE. Mr. T.	BLACK. Mr. M.
1. P. to Q.'s 4th.	1. P. to K.'s 3rd.
2. Kt. to K. B.'s 3rd.	2. P. to Q.'s 4th.
3. P. to Q. B.'s 4th.	3. P. to Q. B.'s 4th. (a)
4. P. to K.'s 3rd.	4. K. Kt. to B.'s 3rd.
5. Kt. to Q. B.'s 3rd.	5. P. to Q. R.'s 3rd.
6. K. B. to Q.'s 3rd.	6. Q. P. takes P.
7. B. takes P.	7. P. to Q. Kt.'s 4th.
8. B. to Q.'s 3rd.	8. Q. B. to Kt.'s 2nd.
9. P. takes P.	9. K. B. takes P.
10. Castles.	10. Q. Kt. to Q.'s 2nd.
11. P. to Q. R.'s 3rd.	11. Q. Kt. to Kt.'s 3rd. (b)
12. Q. to K.'s 2nd. (c)	12. Q. to Q. B.'s 2nd.
13. P. to K. R.'s 3rd.	13. Q. R. to Q.'s sq.
14. P. to Q. Kt.'s 4th.	14. B. to Q.'s 3rd.
15. Q. B. to Kt.'s 2nd.	15. Castles.
16. Q. R. to Q. B.'s sq.	16. Q. to K.'s 2nd.
17. K. B. to Q. Kt.'s sq.	17. P. to K.'s 4th.
18. P. to K.'s 4th.	18. Q. Kt. to B.'s 5th.
19. Q. Kt. to Q.'s 5th.	19. Kt. takes Kt.
20. P. takes Kt.	20. B. takes P.
21. Q. to Q.'s 3rd. (d)	21. P. to K.'s 5th.
22. Q. to Q.'s 4th.	22. Kt. takes Q. B.
23. Q. takes Kt.	23. P. takes Kt.
24. K. R. to K.'s sq.	24. Q. to K. Kt.'s 4th.
25. P. to K. Kt.'s 4th.	25. Q. to K. B.'s 5th.

And white resigned.

(a) The acknowledged best move.
(b) With the intention of capturing the Kt. and doubling his pawns.
(c) Having in view the capture of Kt.'s P.
(d) Miscalculation; white overlooked, by playing Q. to Q.'s 3rd and threatening mate, that black could readily interpose his K.'s P., winning a clear piece; for should white venture to capture the B. he would lose his Q. on the next move.

ALLGAIER GAMBIT.

Played at the Brooklyn Chess-club, between Mr. J. Philip and Mr. W. Horner.

WHITE. Mr. Philip.	BLACK. Mr. Horner.
1. P. to K.'s 4th.	1. P. to K.'s 4th.
2. P. to K. B.'s 4th.	2. P. takes B. P.
3. K. Kt. to B.'s 3rd.	3. P. to K. Kt.'s 4th.
4. P. to K. R.'s 4th.	4. P. to K. Kt.'s 5th.
5. K. Kt. to K.'s 5th.	5. P. to K. R.'s 4th.
6. K. B. to Q. B.'s 4th.	6. K. R. to his 2nd.
7. P. to Q.'s 4th.	7. P. to Q.'s 3rd.
8. K. Kt. to Q.'s 3rd.	8. P. to K. B.'s 6th.
9. P. to K. Kt.'s 3rd.	9. K. B. to K. R.'s 3rd.
10. K. Kt. to K. B.'s 4th.	10. B. takes K. Kt.
11. Q. B. takes B.	11. Q. to K.'s 2nd.
12. Q. to her 3rd.	12. K. R. to his sq. (a)

23

13. Q. Kt. to B.'s 3rd.
14. K. to his B.'s 2nd.
15. P. to Q. R.'s 4th.
16. K. R. to K.'s sq.
17. Q. B. to K. Kt.'s 5th.
18. Kt. to Q.'s 5th. (d)
19. K. P. takes P. (dis. ch.)
20. K. R. takes Kt. (ch.)
21. B. takes Q.
22. R. to K.'s sq. (ch.)
23. Q. to K.'s 3rd.
24. B. to Q.'s 3rd.
25. P. to Q. Kt.'s 3rd.
26. P. to Q. Kt.'s 4th.
27. B. to K.'s 4th.
28. Q. to her B.'s 3rd (ch.)
29. B. to Q.'s 3rd.
30. R. takes R. (ch.)
31. B. takes Kt.
32. K. to B.'s sq.
33. B. to Q.'s 3rd.
34. K. to Kt.'s sq.
35. K. to B.'s sq.

13. P. to Q. B.'s 3rd.
14. P. to Q. R.'s 4th. (b)
15. Q. Kt. to Q.'s 2nd.
16. Q. Kt. to K. B.'s sq.
17. Q. to her B.'s 2nd. (c)
18. B. P. takes Kt.
19. K. Kt. to K.'s 2nd.
20. Q. takes K. R.
21. K. takes B.
22. K. to Q.'s sq.
23. Kt. to K. Kt.'s 3rd
24. B. to Q.'s 2nd.
25. K. to Q. B.'s 2nd.
26. Q. R. to K.'s sq.
27. P. to K. B.'s 4th.
28. K. to Q. Kt.'s sq.
29. P. to K. B.'s 5th.
30. R. takes R.
31. R. to K.'s 7th (ch.)
32. P. takes K. Kt. P.
33. R. to K. R.'s 7th.
34. P. to B.'s 7th (ch.)

And white resigns.

(a) Fearing the advance of white's K.'s P.
(b) Threatening to win B.
(c) Had he played P. to K. B.'s 3rd, white would have replied with P. to K.'s 5th, winning the queen.
(d) This sacrifice gives white a strong attack.

EVANS' GAMBIT.

Game between Messrs. N. Marache and W. D., both of New York.

WHITE. Mr. N. M.

BLACK. Mr. W. D.

1. P. to K.'s 4th.
2. Kt. to K. B.'s 3rd.
3. B. to Q. B.'s 4th.
4. P. to Q. Kt.'s 4th.
5. P. to Q. B.'s 3rd.
6. P. to Q.'s 4th.
7. Castles.
8. Q. to Kt.'s 3rd.
9. B. takes P. (ch.)
10. B. takes Kt.
11. Kt. to Kt.'s 5th.
12. P. takes P.
13. P. to Q.'s 6th.
14. Q. to B.'s 7th (ch.)
15. P. takes Kt.
16. Q. takes R.
17. B. to Q. R.'s 3rd.
18. Q. to B.'s 7th (ch.)
19. B. to Q.'s 6th.
20. Q. to Q. B.'s 7th (ch.)

1. P. to K.'s 4th.
2. Kt. to Q. B.'s 3rd.
3. B. to Q. B.'s 4th.
4. B. takes P.
5. B. to R.'s 4th.
6. P. takes P.
7. B. takes P.
8. B. takes R.
9. K. to Kt.'s sq.
10. R. takes B.
11. P. to Q.'s 4th.
12. Kt. to K.'s 2nd.
13. K. to K.'s sq.
14. K. to Q.'s 2nd.
15. Q. takes P.
16. P. to Q. B.'s 3rd.
17. Q. takes Kt.
18. K. to Q.'s sq.
19. B. to R.'s 6th.

And mates in three moves.

CUNNINGHAM GAMBIT.

Between V. Bilguer and Mr. M——t.

WHITE. V. B.	BLACK. Mr. M.
1. P. to K.'s 4th.	1. P. to K.'s 4th.
2. P. to K. B's 4th.	2. P. takes P.
3. K. Kt. to B.'s 3rd.	3. K. B. to K.'s 2nd.
4. K. B. to Q. B.'s 4th.	4. B. checks.
5. P. to K. Kt.'s 3rd.	5. P. takes P.
6. Castles.	6. P. takes P. (ch.)
7. K. to R.'s sq.	7. P. to Q.'s 3rd.
8. B. takes K. B. P. (ch.)	8. K. takes B.
9. Kt. takes B. (dis. ch.)	9. K. Kt. to B.'s 3rd.
10. P. to Q.'s 4th.	10. Q. B. to K. R.'s 6th.
11. R. to K. B.'s 3rd.	11. B. to K. Kt.'s 5th.
12. R. takes Kt. (ch.)	12. Q. takes R.
13. Q. takes B.	13. Q. to K. B.'s 8th (ch.)
14. K. takes P.	14. Q. takes Q. B.
15. Q. Kt. to B.'s 3rd.	15. Q. takes R.
16. Q. to K. B.'s 5th (ch.)	16. K. to his sq.
17. Q. to Q. B.'s 8th (ch.)	17. K. to his 2nd.
18. Q. takes P. (ch.)	18. K. to his sq.
19. Q. to B.'s 8th (ch.)	19. K. to B.'s 2nd.
20. Q. takes P. (ch.)	20. K. to his sq.
21. Kt. to K. B.'s 5th.	

And must win.

EVANS' GAMBIT.

WHITE. Herr Anderssen.	BLACK. Mr. Perigal.
1. K. P. 2.	1. K. P. 2.
2. K. Kt. to B.'s 3rd.	2. Q. Kt. to B.'s 3rd.
3. K. B. to Q. B.'s 4th.	3. K. B. to Q. B.'s 4th.
4. Q. Kt. P. 2.	4. B. takes P.
5. Q. B. P. 1.	5. B. to Q. B.'s 4th.
6. Castles.	6. Q. P. 1.
7. Q. P. 2.	7. P. takes P.
8. P. takes P.	8. B. to Q. Kt.'s 3rd.
9. K. R. P. 1.	9. K. R. P. 1.
10. Q. Kt. to B.'s 3rd.	10. K. Kt. to K.'s 2nd.
11. Q. P. 1.	11. Q. Kt. to K.'s 4th.
12. Kt. takes Kt.	12. P. takes Kt
13. Q. Kt. to K.'s 2nd.	13. K. B. to Q. B.'s 4th.
14. K. to R.'s sq.	14. K. Kt. P. 2.
15. Q. B. to Kt.'s 2nd.	15. Kt. to K. Kt.'s 3rd.
16 Q. to R.'s 4th (ch.)	16. Q. B. to Q.'s 2nd.
17 Q. to Q. Kt.'s 3rd.	17. K. B. to Q.'s 3rd.
18. Q. R. to K.'s sq. (a)	18. Castles.
19. Q. to K. B.'s 3rd.	19. K. to R.'s 2nd.
20. Q. to K. R.'s 5th.	20. K. B. P. 2.
21. Kt. to K. Kt.'s 3rd.	21. Kt. to B.'s 5th.
22. Q. to Q.'s sq.	22. K. Kt. P. 1. (b)
23. Kt. takes P.	23. Kt. takes Kt.'s P. (c)
24. K. takes Kt.	24. B. takes Kt.
25. P. takes B.	25. Q. to K. R.'s 5th.
26. P. takes P.	26. R. takes P. (d)
27. R. to K.'s 4th. (e)	27. Q. R. to K. Kt.'s sq.
28. K. B. to Q.'s 3rd.	28. K. to R.'s sq.
29. K. B. P. 1. And wins.	

(*a*) Intending to play K. B. P. 2.

(*b*) Up to this point Mr. Perigal plays this game with his accustomed skill, and we do not hesitate to pronounce his game superior to that of his formidable opponent?

(*c*) An unsound sacrifice; he should rather take P. with P., then Kt. with B., followed by Q. to K. R.'s 5th.

(*d*) Very well played; if white takes R. with P., he checks with R. at K. Kt.'s square, then with Q. at Kt.'s 5th, and then takes B.; and if white plays 27. B. to Q.'s 3rd, the reply would be K. P. 1, and wins.

(*e*) The only move, it appears.

QUEEN'S GAMBIT.

BLACK. Mr. Perigal.	WHITE. Herr Anderssen.
1. Q. P. 2.	1. Q. P. 2.
2. Q. B. P. 2.	2. P. takes P.
3. Q. Kt. to B.'s 3rd.	3. K. P. 2.
4. Q. P. 1.	4. K. B. to Q. B.'s 4th.
5. K. P. 1.	5. K. Kt. to B.'s 3rd.
6. B. takes P.	6. Castles.
7. K. Kt. to K.'s 2nd.	7. Q. R. P. 1.
8. Q. R. P. 1.	8. Q. Kt. to Q.'s 2nd.
9. Q. Kt. P. 2.	9. K. B. to R.'s 2nd.
10. Q. B. to Kt.'s 2nd.	10. K. Kt. to Kt.'s 5th.
11. K. Kt. to Kt.'s 3rd.	11. K. B. P. 2.
12. K. R. P. 1.	12. Kt. takes B. P.
13. Q. P. 1 (ch.)	13. K. to R.'s sq.
14. K. takes Kt.	14. Q. to K. R.'s 5th.
15. Q. to K. R.'s 5th.	15. Q. takes B.
16. K. to K.'s sq.	16. K. B. P. 1.
17. K. Kt. to K.'s 4th.	17. B. takes P.
18. Q. R. to Q.'s sq.	18. P. takes P.
19. Kt. takes P.	19. Q. to Q. Kt.'s 6th.
20. B. to Q. R.'s sq.	20. B. to Q.'s 5th.
21. R. to Q.'s 3rd.	21. Kt. to K. B.'s 3rd.
22. Q. to K.'s 2nd.	22. Q. to K.'s 3rd.
23. Kt. takes B.	23. Q. takes Kt.
24. K. to Q.'s 2nd.	24. Q. to K. B.'s 4th.
25. K. R. to Q.'s sq.	25. B. takes Kt. (ch.)
26. B. takes B.	26. K. P. 1.
27. R. to Q.'s 4th.	27. Q. R. to B.'s sq.
28. B. to Q. R.'s sq.	28. K. B. P. 1.
29. Q. to K.'s 3rd.	29. P. takes P.
30. K. to K.'s sq.	30. Q. R. to B.'s 7th.
31. Q. to K. Kt.'s sq.　Resigns.	31. Kt. to K. Kt.'s 5th.

PETROFF'S DEFENCE.

BLACK. Mr. Harrwitz.	WHITE. Mr. Lowenthal.
1. K. P. 2.	1. K. P. 2.
2. K. Kt. to B.'s 3rd.	2. K. Kt. to B.'s 3rd.
3. Q. Kt. to B.'s 3rd.	3. K. B. to Q. Kt.'s 5th.
4. K. B. to Q. B.'s 4th.	4. Q. P. 1.
5. Castles.	5. Castles.
6. Q. P. 1. (*a*)	6. B. takes Kt.
7. P. takes B.	7. K. R. P. 1.
8. K. R. P. 1.	8. Q. Kt. to B.'s 3rd.
9. Kt. to R.'s 2nd.	9. Q. P. 1.
10. P. takes P.	10. Kt. takes P.

11. Q. to K.'s sq. (b)	11. R. to K.'s sq.
12. Q. B. to Q.'s 2nd.	12. R. to B.'s 4th.
13. K. B. P. 1.	18. Q. to Q.'s 8rd.
14. K. Kt. P. 2.	14. B. to K.'s 8rd.
15. Q. to K. B.'s 2nd.	15. Kt. to B.'s 5th.
16. B. takes Kt.	16. P. takes B.
17. B. to Q. Kt.'s 8rd.	17. Q. R. P. 2.
18. K. R. to K.'s sq. (c)	18. Q. R. P. 1.
19. B. takes B.	19. R. takes B.
20. Q. R. P. 1.	20. R. takes R. (ch.)
21. Q. takes R.	21. K. to B.'s sq.
22. Kt. to B.'s sq.	22. R. to K.'s sq.
28. Q. to B.'s 2nd.	28. Q. to K.'s 4th.
24. Q. P. 1.	24. Q. to K.'s 7th.
25. R. to Kt.'s sq.	25. Q. to B.'s 5th.
26. Q. to Q.'s 2nd.	26. R. to K.'s 7th.
27. Q. to Q.'s sq. (d)	27. Q. Kt. P. 1.
28. Kt. to Q.'s 2nd.	28. Q. to R.'s 8rd.
29. Kt. to K.'s 4th.	29. R. to K.'s 6th.
80. K. to B.'s 2nd.	30. Q. to B.'s 5th.
31. Q. to Q.'s 2nd.	81. Q. to Q.'s 4th.
82. R. to K.'s sq. (e)	82. Kt. to R.'s 4th. (f)
88. Q. to B.'s sq.	88. Kt. to B.'s 5th.
84. Q. to Q. Kt.'s sq. (g)	84. R. takes K. B. P. (ch.)
85. K. to Kt.'s 2nd.	85. R. to K.'s 6th. And wins.

Duration, seven hours and a half.

(a) Kt. to Q.'s 5th would have been far better.
(b) Better at once to have played Q. B. to Q.'s 2nd.
(c) Q. R. to Kt.'s sq. would have been the proper move; if, then, white defends his Q. Kt. P., black might play Q. R. P. 2.
(d) Better than to Q.'s 3rd. or taking P.
(e) Q. to Q. B.'s sq. and then Q. to Kt.'s 2nd looks more promising, since if the Kt. moved, white would lose his Q. R. P.
(f) Well played; this brings his Kt. into a very commanding position.
(g) An unaccountable oversight.

SICILIAN OPENING.

Between Messrs. Anderssen and Staunton.

WHITE. Mr. A.	BLACK. Mr. S.
1. P. to K.'s 4th.	1. P. to Q. B.'s 4th.
2. P. to Q.'s 4th.	2. P. takes P.
8. Kt. to K. B.'s 8rd.	8. P. to K.'s 8rd.
4. Kt takes P.	4. B. to Q. B.'s 4th.
5. Kt. to Q. B.'s 8rd.	5. P. to Q. R.'s 8rd.
6. B. to K.'s 8rd.	6. B. to Q. R.'s 2nd.
7. B. to Q.'s 8rd.	7. Kt. to K.'s 2nd.
8. Castles.	8. Castles.
9. Q. to K. R.'s 5th.	9. Kt. to K. Kt.'s 3rd.
10. P. to K.'s 5th.	10. Q. to her B.'s 2nd.
11. Q. R. to K.'s sq.	11. P. to Q. Kt.'s 4th.
12. P. to K. B.'s 4th.	12. B. to Q. Kt.'s 2nd.
18. Kt. to K.'s 4th.	18. Q. B. takes Kt.
14. B. takes B.	14. Kt. to Q. B.'s 3rd.
15. Kt. takes Kt.	15. P. takes Kt.
16. P. to K. Kt.'s 4th.	16. Q. R. to Q.'s sq.
17. K. to R.'s sq.	17. P. to Q. B.'s 4th.
18. R. to K. B.'s 8rd.	18. Q. to Q. R.'s 4th.

23*

19. Q. R. to K. B.'s sq.
20. B. to Q.'s 3rd.
21. R. to K. R.'s 3rd.
22. P. to K. Kt.'s 5th.
23. P. takes R.
24. Q. R. to K. B.'s 3rd.
25. P. takes P.
26. P. checks.
27. Q. to Kt.'s 5th.
28. Q. checks.
29. P. to K. B.'s 5th.
30. B. to K. R.'s 6th.
31. K. moves.
32. R. to K. B.'s 2nd.

19. Q. to R.'s 5th.
20. Q. takes Q. R. P.
21. P. to K. R.'s 3rd.
22. R. takes B.
23. Q. checks.
24. Kt. to K.'s 2nd.
25. P. to K. Kt.'s 3rd.
26. K. to R.'s sq.
27. Kt. to K. B.'s 4th.
28. Kt. to Kt.'s 2nd.
29. Q. to Q. Kt.'s 6th.
30. Q. to Q.'s 8th (ch.)
31. Q. to K.'s 7th (ch.)
And black resigns.

PHILIDOR'S DEFENCE.
By Philidor.

WHITE.	BLACK.
1. P. to K.'s 4th.	1. P. to K.'s 4th.
2. K. Kt. to B.'s 3rd.	2. P. to Q.'s 3rd.
3. P. to Q.'s 4th.	3. P. to K. B.'s 4th.
4. P. takes K.'s P.	4. K. B. P. takes K. P.
5. Kt. to Kt.'s 5th.	5. P. to Q.'s 4th.
6. P. to K. B.'s 4th.	6. K. B. to Q. B.'s 4th.
7. P. to Q. B.'s 4th.	7. P. to Q. B.'s 3rd.
8. Q. Kt. to B.'s 3rd.	8. K. Kt. to K.'s 2nd.
9. P. to K. R.'s 4th.	9. P. to K. R.'s 3rd.
10. K. Kt. to R.'s 3rd.	10. Castles.
11. Q. Kt. to Q. R.'s 4th.	11. B. to Q. Kt.'s 5th (ch.)
12. B. to Q.'s 2nd.	12. B. takes B. (ch.)
13. Q. takes B.	13. P. to Q.'s 5th.
14. P. to Q. B.'s 5th.	14. P. to Q. Kt.'s 4th.
15. P. takes P. (in passing).	15. Q. R.'s P. takes P.
16. P. to Q. Kt.'s 3rd.	16. Q. B. to K.'s 3rd.
17. B. to K.'s 2nd.	17. Kt. to K. B.'s 4th.
18. K. Kt. to his sq.	18. K. Kt. to Kt.'s 6th.
19. K. R. to his 2nd.	19. P. to K.'s 6th.
20. Q. to her Kt.'s 2nd.	20. P. to Q.'s 6th.
21. B. to K. B.'s 3rd.	21. K.'s R. takes P.
22. Castles on Q.'s side.	22. K.'s R. takes Kt.
23. P. takes K. R.	23. Q.'s R. takes P.
24. P. to Q. R.'s 3rd.	24. R. to Q. B.'s 5th (ch.)
25. K. to Q. Kt.'s sq.	25. R. to Q. B.'s 7th.
26. Q. to Kt.'s 4th.	26. Q. Kt. to R.'s 3rd.
27. Q. to K. B.'s 4th.	27. Q. Kt. to B.'s 4th.
28. Q. takes K. Kt.	

And black mates in two moves.

SALVIO GAMBIT.
Between Messrs. V. H. der Laza and H., of Berlin.

WHITE. Mr. H.	BLACK. V. H. der L.
1. P. to K.'s 4th.	1. P. to K.'s 4th.
2. P. to K. B.'s 4th.	2. P. takes P.
3. K. Kt. to B.'s 3rd.	3. P. to K. Kt.'s 4th.
4. K. B. to Q. B.'s 4th.	4. P. to K. Kt.'s 5th.

5. Kt. to K.'s 5th.
6. K. to B.'s sq.
7. P. to Q.'s 4th.
8. P. to K. Kt.'s 3rd.
9. K. to B.'s 2nd.
10. K. to his 3rd.
11. Kt. to Q.'s 3rd.
12. Kt. to K. B.'s 4th.
13. K. to Q.'s 3rd.
14. Q. B. takes B.
15. Q. Kt. to B.'s 3rd.
16. Q. B. to Q.'s 6th.
17. B. takes Kt. (ch.)
18. P. to K. R.'s 3rd.
19. B. takes Q. Kt. P.
20. K. to his 3rd.
21. Q. to K. Kt.'s sq.
22. Q. takes P. (ch.)
23. Q. takes doubled P.

5. Q. to R.'s 5th (ch.)
6. K. Kt. to R.'s 3rd.
7. P. to K. B.'s 6th.
8. Q. to R.'s 6th (ch.)
9. Q. to K. Kt.'s 7th (ch.)
10. P. to K. B.'s 3rd.
11. K. Kt. to B.'s 2nd.
12. K. B. to K. R.'s 3rd.
13. B. takes Kt.
14. P. to Q. B.'s 3rd.
15. Castles.
16. P. to Q. Kt.'s 4th.
17. R. takes B.
18. P. to Q. Kt.'s 5th.
19. Q. B. to R.'s 3rd (ch.)
20. Q. takes K. Kt.'s P.
21. Q. to her B.'s 2nd.
22. R. to K. Kt.'s 2nd.

And wins.

COCHRANE GAMBIT.

Between Messrs. La Bourdonnais and Cochrane.

WHITE. M. La B.

1. P. to K.'s 4th.
2. P. to K. B.'s 4th.
3. K. Kt. to B.'s 3rd.
4. K. B. to Q. B.'s 4th.
5. Kt. to K.'s 5th.
6. K. to B.'s sq.
7. P. to K. Kt.'s 3rd.
8. K. to B.'s 2nd.
9. K. to his 3rd.
10. K. to Q.'s 3rd.
11. B. takes P.
12. P. to Q. B.'s 3rd.
13. B. takes K. B. P. (ch.)
14. K. B. to Q. Kt.'s 3rd.
15. K. to B.'s 2nd.
16. Q. to K. B.'s sq.
17. Q. takes Q.
18. P. to Q.'s 3rd.
19. R. to K. Kt.'s sq.
20. Q. B. takes B.
21. R. takes P.
22. Kt. takes Kt.
23. K. to B.'s sq.
24. Q. Kt. to Q.'s 2nd.
25. K. B. to Q.'s sq.
26. K. R. to Kt.'s sq.
27. P. to Q. Kt.'s 3rd.
28. R. takes B.
29. Kt. takes Kt.
30. K. takes R.

BLACK. Mr. C.

1. P. to K.'s 4th.
2. P. takes P.
3. P. to K. Kt.'s 4th.
4. P. to K. Kt.'s 5th.
5. Q. to K. R.'s 5th (ch.)
6. P. to K. B.'s 6th.
7. Q. to K. R.'s 6th (ch.)
8. Q. to Kt.'s 7th (ch.)
9. B. to K. R.'s 3rd (ch.)
10. P. to Q.'s 4th.
11. Q. Kt. to R.'s 3rd.
12. P. to Q. B.'s 3rd.
13. K. to his 2nd.
14. Q. Kt. to B.'s 4th (ch.)
15. Q. Kt. takes K. P.
16. Q. B. to K. B.'s 4th.
17. Kt. to B.'s 7th (dis. ch.)
18. P. takes Q.
19. Q. R. to Q.'s sq.
20. K. Kt. takes B.
21. Kt. takes Q.'s P.
22. B. takes Kt. (ch.)
23. K. R. to B.'s sq.
24. K. Kt. to B.'s 4th.
25. Kt. to K.'s 6th.
26. B. to K. B.'s 8th.
27. K. R. to B.'s 7th.
28. Kt. takes R.
29. Q. R. takes B. (ch.)
30. R. takes Kt. (ch.)

And wins.

CENTRE COUNTER-GAMBIT.

Between Mr. H. of Berlin and V. H. der Laza.

WHITE. Mr. H.	BLACK. V. H. der L.
1. P. to K.'s 4th.	1. P. to Q.'s 4th.
2. P. takes P.	2. K. Kt. to B.'s 3rd.
3. B. checks.	3. B. to Q.'s 2nd.
4. B. to Q. B.'s 4th.	4. P. to Q. Kt.'s 4th.
5. B. to Q. Kt.'s 3rd.	5. B. to K. Kt.'s 5th.
6. P. to K. B.'s 3rd.	6. B. to his own sq.
7. Q. to K.'s 2nd.	7. P. to Q. R.'s 3rd.
8. P. to Q. B.'s 4th.	8. P. to Q. B.'s 3rd.
9. Q. Kt. to B.'s 3rd.	9. P. takes Q.'s P.
10. P. takes Q.'s P.	10. B. to Q. Kt.'s 2nd.
11. Q. to K.'s 5th.	11. Q. Kt. to Q.'s 2nd.
12. Q. to her 4th.	12. Q. to her Kt.'s 3rd.
13. Q. to K.'s 3rd.	13. P. to Q. Kt.'s 5th.
14. Kt. to Q. R.'s 4th.	14. Q. to her R.'s 4th.
15. P. to Q.'s 6th.	15. Q. B. to his 3rd.
16. P. to Q. R.'s 3rd.	16. P. to K.'s 3rd.
17. Q. R. P. takes P.	17. Q. takes P.
18. Q. to her B.'s 3rd.	18. Q. takes P.
19. P. to Q.'s 4th.	19. K. Kt. to Q.'s 4th.
20. B. takes Kt.	20. Q. takes B.
21. K. Kt. to K.'s 2nd.	21. B. to Q. Kt.'s 4th.
22. K. Kt. to K. B.'s 4th	22. Q. to K. B.'s 4th.
23. K. to B.'s 2nd.	23. K. B. to Q.'s 3rd.
24. P. to K. Kt.'s 4th.	24. Q. to K. B.'s 3rd.
25. Q. to K.'s 3rd.	25. Castles on K.'s side.
26. P. to K. R.'s 4th	26. P. to K.'s 4th.
27. K. Kt. to R.'s 5th.	27. Q. to K. Kt.'s 3rd.
28. Q. to K.'s 4th.	28. P. to K. B.'s 4th.
29. Q. to her 5th (ch.)	29. K. to R.'s sq.
30. P. to K. Kt.'s 5th.	30. P. to K. B.'s 5th.
31. K. R. to Q.'s sq.	31. Q. takes Kt.
32. Q takes K. B.	32. Q. takes K. R. P. (ch.)
33. K. to Kt.'s sq.	33. Q. takes P. (ch.)
34. K. to R.'s sq.	34. Q. to R.'s 5th (ch.)
35. K. to Kt.'s 2nd.	35. Q. to Kt.'s 6th (ch.)
36. K. to R.'s sq.	36. K. R. to B.'s 4th

And white loses the game.

IRREGULAR OPENING.

Between Mr. Horwitz and Mr. Staunton.

WHITE. Mr. H.	BLACK. Mr. S.
1. P. to K.'s 4th.	1. P. to Q. B.'s 4th.
2. P. to K. B.'s 4th.	2. P. to K.'s 3rd.
3. K. Kt. to B.'s 3rd.	3. P. to Q.'s 4th.
4. P. takes P.	4. P. takes P.
5. K. B. to K.'s 2nd.	5. K. B. to Q.'s 3rd.
6. P. to Q. B.'s 3rd.	6. Q. Kt. to B.'s 3rd.
7. P. to Q.'s 3rd.	7. Q. to B.'s 2nd.
8. P. to K. Kt.'s 3rd.	8. K. Kt. to B.'s 3rd.
9. Q. Kt. to R.'s 3rd.	9. P. to Q. R.'s 3rd.
10. Q. Kt. to B.'s 2nd.	10. Castles.
11. P. to Q.'s 4th.	11. K. R. to K.'s sq.
12. Castles.	12. Q. B. to Q.'s 2nd.

13. K. to Kt.'s 2nd.
14. K. R. to K.'s sq.
15. K. B. to his sq.
16. R. takes R.
17. P. to Q. Kt.'s 3rd
18. Q. Kt. takes P.
19. K. B. to Q.'s 3rd.
20. Q. B. to Kt.'s 2nd
21. Q. to B.'s 2nd.
22. Kt. takes B.
23. P. takes Kt.
24. Q. to Q. Kt.'s sq.
25. K. to Kt.'s sq.
26. Q. to K.'s sq.
27. R. to Q. B.'s sq.
28. K. B. to B.'s sq.
29. P. takes P.
30. Q. to her 2nd.
31. R. to B.'s 8th.
32. R. to Q.'s 8th.
33. Q. to K. B.'s 4th.
34. K. to Kt.'s 2nd.
35. R. to K. Kt.'s 8th (ch.)

13. K. R. to K.'s 2nd.
14. Q. R. to K.'s sq.
15. Q. to her Kt.'s 3rd.
16. R. takes R.
17. P. takes Q. P.
18. Q. B. to K. Kt.'s 5th.
19. K. Kt. to K.'s 5th.
20. K. B. to Q. B.'s 4th.
21. K. B. takes Q. Kt.
22. Kt. takes Kt.
23. R. to Q. B.'s 2nd.
24. Q. B. to K. B.'s 6th (ch.)
25. P. to K. B.'s 4th.
26. R. to K.'s 2nd.
27. K. to B.'s 2nd.
28. P. to K. Kt.'s 4th.
29. K. Kt. takes P. at his 4th.
30. K. to Kt.'s 3rd.
31. Q. to K.'s 3rd.
32. B. to K. Kt.'s 5th.
33. Kt. to K. B.'s 6th (ch.)
34. Q. to K.'s 8th.
35. K. to R.'s 4th.

White surrenders.

IRREGULAR OPENING.

Between Mr. Staunton and M. St. Amant.

WHITE. Mr. S.

BLACK. M. St. A.

1. P. to Q. B.'s 4th.
2. P. to K.'s 4th.
3. P. to Q.'s 4th.
4. K. P. takes P.
5. Q. Kt. to B.'s 3rd.
6. K. Kt. to B.'s 3rd.
7. K. B. to Q.'s 3rd.
8. Castles.
9. Q. B. to K.'s 3rd.
10. P. to Q. Kt.'s 3rd.
11. K. to R.'s sq.
12. Q. Kt. to K.'s 2nd.
13. Q. B. to K. B.'s 4th.
14. Kt. takes B.
15. Q. Kt. takes Kt.
16. K. B. to K.'s 2nd.
17. K. R. to K.'s sq.
18. Kt. to his sq.
19. R. takes B.
20. Q. to her 3rd.
21. Kt. to B.'s 3rd.
22. P. to K. R.'s 3rd.
23. Kt. to K.'s 5th.
24. R. takes R.
25. R. takes R. (ch.)
26. K. to Kt.'s sq.
27. R. to K.'s 2nd.
28. Q. R. to Q.'s sq.
29. K. R. to Q.'s 2nd.
30. P. to Q. R.'s 4th. Resigned.

1. P. to K.'s 3rd.
2. P. to Q. B.'s 3rd.
3. P. to Q.'s 4th.
4. K. P. takes P.
5. K. Kt. to B.'s 3rd.
6. K. B. to K.'s 2nd.
7. Castles.
8. Q. B. to K. Kt.'s 5th.
9. Q. Kt. to Q.'s 2nd.
10. P. to K. R.'s 3rd.
11. K. B. to Q. Kt.'s 5th.
12. K. B. to Q.'s 3rd.
13. B. takes B.
14. K. Kt. to K. R.'s 4th.
15. B. takes Q. Kt.
16. K. R. to K.'s sq.
17. Q. to her B.'s 2nd.
18. B takes B.
19. Kt. to K. B.'s 3rd.
20. Kt. to K. Kt.'s 5th.
21. K. R. to K.'s 5th.
22. Q. R. to K. R.'s sq.
23. Kt. takes Kt.
24. Kt. takes Q.
25. K. to R.'s 2nd.
26. Q. to K. B.'s 5th.
27. Q. takes Q. P.
28. P. takes P.
29. P. to Q. Kt.'s 4th.
30. P. to Q. R.'s 3rd.

GAMES AT ODDS.

SICILIAN GAME.

Mr. Staunton gives the odds of the pawn and move to Mr. Buckle.

[In each of these two games, the king's bishop's pawn of white must be cmoved.]

BLACK. Mr. B.	WHITE. Mr. S.
1. P. to K.'s 4th.	1. Q. Kt. to B.'s 3rd.
2. P. to Q.'s 4th.	2. P. to Q.'s 4th.
3. P. to K.'s 5th.	3. Q. B. to K.'s 3rd.
4. K. Kt. to B.'s 3rd.	4. Q. B. to K. Kt.'s 5th.
5. Q. B. to K.'s 3rd.	5. P. to K.'s 3rd.
6. K. B. to Q.'s 3rd.	6. Q. to K.'s 2nd.
7. Q. Kt. to Q.'s 2nd.	7. P. to K. Kt.'s 3rd.
8. P. to K. R.'s 3rd.	8. B. takes Kt.
9. Kt. takes B.	9. B. to R.'s 3rd.
10. Q. to her 2nd.	10. B. takes B.
11. Q. takes B.	11. Q. checks.
12. P. to Q. B.'s 3rd.	12. Q. takes Kt. P.
13. Castles.	13. Q. to her R.'s 6th.
14. Kt. to K. Kt.'s 5th.	14. Q. to K.'s 2nd.
15. B. to K.'s 2nd.	15. K. Kt. to R.'s 3rd.
16. Q. to her 2nd.	16. K. Kt. to B.'s 4th.
17. Q. R. to Kt.'s sq.	17. P. to Q. Kt.'s 3rd.
18. B. to Q. Kt's 5th.	18. Q. to her 2nd.
19. P. to Q. B.'s 4th.	19. P. to Q. R.'s 3rd.
20. P. takes Q. P.	20. P. takes B.
21. P. takes Kt.	21. Q. takes Q. B. P.
22. Q. to K. B.'s 4th.	22. Q. R. to his 5th.
23. K. R. to Q.'s sq.	23. Castles.
24. Kt. to K.'s 4th.	24. K. to Kt.'s 2nd.
25. Kt. to B.'s 6th.	25. Q. R. to B.'s 5th.
26. P. to K. R.'s 4th.	26. Kt. to K.'s 2nd.
27. Q. to Kt.'s 5th.	27. Kt. to Q.'s 4th.
28. Kt. to Kt.'s 4th.	28. Kt. to K. B.'s 5th.
29. P. to Q.'s 5th.	29. Kt. takes P.
30 Q. to R.'s 6th (ch.)	30. K. to Kt.'s sq.
31 Kt. to B.'s 6th (ch.)	31. R. takes Kt.
32 P. takes R.	32. Kt. takes P.
33 R. checks.	33. Kt. to K.'s sq.
34. Q. R. to Q.'s sq.	34. K. to K. Kt.'s 5th.
35. P. to K. Kt.'s 3rd.	35. R. to Q. B.'s 5th.
36. K. R. to Q.'s 7th. And wins.	

Between the same players, at the same odds.

BLACK. Mr. B.	WHITE. Mr. S.
1. P. to K.'s 4th.	1. Q. Kt. to B.'s 3rd.
2. P. to Q.'s 4th.	2. P. to Q.'s 4th.
3. P. to K.'s 5th.	3. B. to K. B.'s 4th.
4. P. to K. Kt.'s 4th.	4. B. to K. Kt.'s 3rd.
5. P. to K. R.'s 4th.	5. P. to K.'s 3rd.

6. P. to K. R.'s 5th.
7. P. to K. B.'s 4th.
8. R. P. takes P.
9. B. to Q.'s 3rd.
10. Q. takes B.
11. P. to K. B.'s 5th.
12. Q. to K. R.'s 3rd.
13. P. takes K. P.
14. Kt. to K.'s 2nd.
15. Kt. to K. B.'s 4th.
16. Kt. takes K. R. P.
17. P. to Q. B.'s 3rd.
18. K. to Q.'s sq.

6. B. to K. B.'s 2nd.
7. P. to K. Kt.'s 3rd.
8. B. takes P.
9. B. takes B.
10. Kt. to K. R.'s 3rd.
11. Kt. takes Kt. P.
12. P. to K. R.'s 4th.
13. Q. to K.'s 2nd.
14. Q. takes P.
15. Q. to B.'s 4th.
16. Castles.
17. Q. to K.'s 5th (ch.)
18. Q. takes R. (ch.)

And black resigned.

Herr Harrwitz plays two games simultaneously without seeing the board or men in either game—one game against Messrs. Henderson, Mathews, and Westland, and one as follows, both of which he won, giving P. and two moves.

Herr Harrwitz against Messrs. Baker, Smith, and Dr. Geddes, in consultation.

[Remove black king's bishop's pawn from the board.]

WHITE. The Allies.

1. K. P. 2.
2. Q. P. 2.
3. K. B. to Q.'s 3rd.
4. K. Kt. to B.'s 3rd.
5. Kt. takes P.
6. Q. B. P. 1.
7. Castles.
8. Q. to K.'s 2nd.
9. Q. Kt. to Q.'s 2nd.
10. Q. Kt. to Q. Kt.'s 3rd.
11. K. B. P. 2.
12. K. P. 1.
13. Q. to K. Kt.'s 4th.
14. Kt. takes Kt.
15. P. takes P.
16. Q. B. to K. B.'s 4th.
17. Q. R. to K.'s sq.
18. Q. Kt. P. 1.
19. B. to Q.'s 2nd.
20. R. takes R.
21. K. to R.'s sq.
22. Q. to K. Kt.'s 3rd.
23. Kt. to K. B.'s 3rd.
24. Q. B. P. 1.
25. R. takes B.
26. B. to K. B.'s 4th.
27. R. takes B.
28. Q. to K. B.'s 2nd.
29. R. to K.'s 4th.
30. R. to K.'s sq.

BLACK. Herr Harrwitz.

1.
2. K. P. 1.
3. Q. B. P. 2.
4. P. takes P.
5. Q. to Q. R.'s 4th (ch.)
6. Kt. to Q. B.'s 3rd.
7. Q. R. P. 1.
8. K. Kt. P. 1. (a)
9. B. to K. Kt.'s 2nd.
10. Q. to Q. B.'s 2nd.
11. K. Kt. to K.'s 2nd.
12. Q. P. 1.
13. Kt. takes Kt.
14. P. takes P.
15. Q. B. to Q.'s 2nd.
16. Castles on K.'s side.
17. Q. to Q. Kt.'s 3rd.
18. Kt. to Q.'s 4th.
19. R. takes R. (ch.)
20. R. to K.'s sq.
21. Kt. to K.'s 2nd.
22. Q. to Q. B.'s 2nd.
23. B. to Q. B.'s 3rd.
24. B. takes Kt.
25. B. takes P.
26. B. takes B.
27. Kt. to B.'s 4th.
28. Q. to K.'s 4th.
29. Q. to Q. R.'s 8th (ch.)
30. Q. to Q.'s 5th.

31. Q. takes Q.	31. Kt. takes Q.
32. B. to K.'s 4th.	32. Q. Kt. P. 1.
33. K. R. P. 1.	33. K. to B.'s 2nd.
34. K. to R.'s 2nd.	34. K. to K.'s 2nd.
35. K. R. P. 1.	35. Kt. to B.'s 4th.
36. K. R. P. 1.	36. K. to B.'s 3rd.
37. K. Kt. P. 2.	37. Kt. to Q.'s 3rd.
38. K. to K. Kt.'s 3rd.	38. R. to Q.'s sq. (b)
39. P. takes P.	39. Kt. takes B. (ch.)
40. R. takes Kt.	40. P. takes P.
41. R. to K.'s 8rd.	41. R. to Q.'s 7th.
42. Q. R. P. 2.	42. K. Kt. P. 1.
43. K. to B.'s 3rd. (c)	43. R. to K. R.'s 7th.
44. K. to Kt.'s 3rd.	44. R. to Q. Kt.'s 7th.
45. K. to B.'s 3rd.	45. K. P. 1.
46. K. to K.'s 4th.	46. K. to K.'s 3rd.
47. K. to B.'s 3rd.	47. Q. R. P. 1.
48. K. to K.'s 4th.	48. R. to K. B.'s 7th (d)
49. R. to K. B.'s 3rd. (e)	49. R. to K. Kt.'s 7th.
50. K. to K.'s 3rd.	50. R. takes P.
51. K. to K.'s 2nd.	51. K. P. 1.

And white resigned. This game lasted nearly six hours.

(*a*) To prevent the attack which white threatens by checking with Q. after pushing on K.'s P.

(*b*) With the intention of taking B. with Kt., and afterwards playing R. to Q.'s 7th.

(*c*) From this point white endeavors, if possible, to draw the game.

(*d*) Black's manœuvring with the rook is highly ingenious.

(*e*) K. to Q.'s 3rd is the correct move, but the game is already lost, as white cannot prevent his antagonist from gaining the K. Kt.'s P.

Herr Harrwitz was the victor in both games; and this result was not the .ess astonishing to the on-lookers from the fact that during the games the talented player, who sat out of sight of the boards, entered freely into conversation with several gentlemen, and amused himself by reading Lever's novel of the Dodd Family Abroad!

Mr. Staunton gives Mr. Stanley, of the New York Chess-club, the odds of pawn and two moves.

[Remove white king's bishop's pawn from the board.]

BLACK. Mr. Stanley.	WHITE. Mr. Staunton.
1. P. to K.'s 4th.	1.
2. P. to Q.'s 4th.	2. P. to K.'s 3rd.
3. K. B. to Q.'s 3rd.	3. P. to Q. B.'s 4th.
4. P. to K.'s 5th.	4. P. to K. Kt.'s 3rd.
5. P. to Q. B.'s 3rd.	5. Q. Kt. to B.'s 3rd.
6. K. Kt. to B.'s 3rd.	6. P. to Q.'s 3rd.
7. P. to K. R.'s 4th.	7. Q. B. P. takes P.
8. Q. B. P. takes P.	8. Q. P. takes K. P.
9. P. to K. R.'s 5th.	9. B. to K. Kt.'s 2nd.
10. R. P. takes P.	10. P. to K. R.'s 3rd.
11. Q. P. takes P.	11. Q. Kt. takes P.
12. B. to Q. Kt.'s 5th (ch.)	12. Q. Kt. to Q.'s 2nd.
13. Castles.	13. K. Kt. to K.'s 2nd.
14. Q. to K.'s 2nd.	14. Q. to Q. Kt.'s 3rd.
15. Q. Kt. to R.'s 3rd.	15. Castles.
16. Q. Kt. to B.'s 4th.	16. Q. takes B.

17. Q. takes P. (ch.)
18. Q. Kt. to Q.'s 6th.
19. Q. takes K. Kt.
20. P. takes Kt.
21. Kt. to K. B.'s 7th (ch.)
22. Q. takes R.
23. B. takes K. R. P.
24. Q. takes Q. B.
25. Q. to K.'s 6th.
26. Q. to Q. B.'s 8th (ch.)
27. K. R. to K.'s sq.
28. K. to B.'s sq.
29. Q. to K.'s 6th.
30. Q. to K.'s 5th (ch.)
31. Q. to K. B.'s 5th.
32. R. to K.'s 8th (ch.)
33. Q. to K. Kt.'s 4th.
34. Q. to K. Kt.'s sq.
35. Q. R. to K.'s sq.
36. R. takes B. (ch.)
37. Q. takes R. (ch.)
38. K. R. to K. B.'s 4th.
39. K. to his Kt.'s 2nd.
40. Q. R. to K. Kt.'s sq.
41. K. to B.'s sq. (dis. ch.)
42. P. to Q. R.'s 4th.
43. Q. R. to K. Kt.'s 2nd.
44. K. to K.'s 2nd.
45. K. R. takes P.
46. K. R. to K. Kt.'s 4th.

17. K. to R.'s sq.
18. Q. Kt. to K.'s 4th.
19. Q. Kt. takes Kt. (ch.)
20. Q. to K. R.'s 4th.
21. R. takes Kt.
22. B. to K. B.'s 4th.
23. Q. takes B.
24. R. to K. B.'s sq.
25. R. to K. B.'s 3rd.
26. B. interposes.
27. R. takes P. (ch.)
28. R. to K. Kt.'s sq.
29. R. to K. Kt.'s 3rd.
30. B. to K. Kt.'s 2nd.
31. R. to K. B.'s 3rd.
32. B. interposes.
33. Q. to R.'s 8th (ch.)
34. Q. to K. R.'s 4th.
35. R. to K. Kt.'s 3rd.
36. K. to Kt.'s 2nd.
37. Q. takes Q.
38. Q. to Q.'s 6th (ch.)
39. Q. to Q. Kt.'s 4th.
40. Q. to K. R.'s 4th.
41. K. to R.'s 2nd.
42. P. to Q. Kt.'s 4th.
43. Q. to K. R.'s 8th (ch.)
44. P. takes R.'s P.
45. P. to Q. R.'s 3rd.

And in a few moves white surrendered.

KING'S BISHOP'S OPENING.

Mr. Staunton gives Mr. Wiel the odds of the queen's knight.

[Remove black's queen's knight from the board.]

BLACK. Mr. S.	WHITE. Mr. W.
1. P. to K.'s 4th.	1. P. to K.'s 4th.
2. K. B. to Q. B.'s 4th.	2. K. B. to Q. B.'s 4th.
3. P. to Q.'s 4th.	3. B. takes Q. P.
4. P. to K. B.'s 4th.	4. B. takes Kt.
5. R. takes B.	5. Q. to K. R.'s 5th (ch.)
6. P. to K. Kt.'s 3rd.	6. Q. takes K. R. P.
7. Q. B. to K.'s 3rd.	7. K. Kt. to B.'s 3rd.
8. P. takes P.	8. Kt. takes K. P.
9. B. takes K. B. P. (ch.)	9. K. takes B.
10. Q. to her 5th (ch.)	10. K. to his sq.
11. Q. takes Kt.	11. Q. Kt. to B.'s 3rd.
12. Castles.	12. P. to Q. Kt.'s 3rd.
13. Q. to K. Kt.'s 4th.	13. Kt. takes K. P.
14. Q. takes K. Kt. P.	14. Kt. to K. B.'s 2nd.
15. Q. R. to K.'s sq.	

And white surrendered.

EVANS' GAMBIT.

Mr. Staunton gives Mr. Harrwitz the odds of queen's rook, Mr. H. playing this game and another at the same time with Mr. Kieseritzky, without seeing the board or men in either game.

[Before playing over this game, remove black's Q.'s R. from the board.]

BLACK. Mr. S.	WHITE. Mr. H.
1. P. to K.'s 4th.	1. P. to K.'s 4th.
2. K. Kt. to B.'s 3rd.	2. Q. Kt. to B.'s 3rd.
3. K. B. to Q. B.'s 4th.	3. K. B. to Q. B.'s 4th.
4. P. to Q. Kt.'s 4th.	4. B. takes Q. Kt. P.
5. P. to Q. B.'s 3rd.	5. B. to R.'s 4th.
6. Castles.	6. P. to Q.'s 3rd.
7. P. to Q.'s 4th.	7. P. takes P.
8. Kt. takes P.	8. K. Kt. to B.'s 3rd.
9. Q. to her R.'s 4th.	9. K. B. to Q. Kt.'s 3rd.
10. P. to K.'s 5th.	10. P. takes P.
11. Kt. takes Q.'s Kt.	11. P. takes Kt.
12. Q. B. to Q. R.'s 3rd.	12. Q. B. to Q.'s 2nd.
13. Q. to her Kt.'s 3rd.	13. Kt. to Q.'s 4th.
14. B. takes Kt.	14. P. takes B.
15. Q. takes P.	15. Q. B. to K.'s 3rd.
16. Q. to her B.'s 6th (ch.)	16. B. to Q.'s 2nd.
17. Q. to her 5th.	17. P. to K. B.'s 3rd. (a)
18. R. to Q.'s sq.	18. Q. to Q. B.'s sq. (b)
19. Q. Kt. to Q.'s 2nd.	19. Q. B. to K.'s 3rd.
20. Q. to B.'s 6th (ch.)	20. K. to B.'s 2nd.
21. Q. to K.'s 4th.	21. Q. B. to K. B.'s 4th.
22. Q. to Q Kt.'s 4th.	22. K. R. to K.'s sq.
23. Kt. to Q. B.'s 4th.	23. Q. R. to Q. Kt.'s sq.
24. Q. to R.'s 4th.	24. Q. to K.'s 3rd.
25. P. to K. R.'s 3rd.	25. Q. R. to Q.'s sq.
26. R. to K.'s sq.	26. Q. R. to Q.'s 6th.
27. Kt. takes B.	27. Q. R. P. takes Kt.
28. P. to K. Kt.'s 4th.	28. B. to K. Kt.'s 3rd.
29. P. to K. B.'s 4th.	29. Q. takes Q. R. P.
30. Q. to her B.'s 6th.	30. Q. takes B.
31. P. to K. B.'s 5th.	31. Q. to her B.'s 4th (ch.)
32. Q. takes Q.	32. P. takes Q.
33. P. takes B. (ch.)	33. K. takes P.
34. K. to Kt.'s 2nd.	34. R. takes Q. B. P.
35. R. to Q.'s sq.	35. K. R. to Q. R.'s sq.
36. R. to Q.'s 2nd.	36. K. R. to Q. R.'s 6th.
37. P. to K. R.'s 4th.	37. Q. R. to K. Kt.'s 6th (ch.)
38. K. to R.'s 2nd.	38. R. takes K. Kt. P.
39. P. to K. R.'s 5th (ch.)	39. K. takes P.
40. R. to Q. B.'s 2nd.	40. K. to R.'s 5th.
41. K. to R.'s sq.	41. K. R. to R.'s 6th (ch.)
42. R. to K. R.'s 2nd.	42. Q. R. to K. B.'s 5th.
43. K. to Kt.'s sq.	43. R. takes R.
44. K. takes R.	

And Mr. Harrwitz announced mate in four more moves.

(a) Conceive the mental labor of Mr. Harrwitz in baffling such an attack as black has maintained, and carrying on a still more arduous game at the same time, and all without the aid of even a chequered board!

(b) These are the best possible moves, we believe.

GAME PLAYED BETWEEN THE EMPEROR NAPOLEON AND THE AUTOMATON CHESS-PLAYER.

When Napoleon entered Berlin, in 1806, somebody thought of the neglected Turk, and Mr. Mælzel, a clever mechanician, was ordered to inspect and repair the dusty old enigma. From cob-webbed dreams of King Fritz and the brave empress, the veteran chess-player awakened to encounter a greater than they, fresh from the field of recent victories. On this remarkable meeting we may dwell for a moment, since its history has been faithfully preserved by an eye-witness, and has never before met the public view.

The emperor, on this occasion, signified his wish to do battle with the Turk; and accordingly Mælzel arranged a second table, near that of the Turk, proposing to repeat the moves on both tables. This was Mælzel's usual mode of exhibition. Napoleon, characteristically overstepping the barrier which separated the Turk from the audience, struck his hand on the automaton's Chess-board, and exclaimed—"I will not contend at a distance! We fight face to face." A grave nod indicated the Turk's assent, and the game began. The emperor was disastrously vanquished. Shortly afterwards, a second exhibition was ordered. On this memorable occasion, the emperor placed a large magnet on the automaton's board. Mælzel smilingly moved the iron, so as not to embarrass the game. The Turk played on with his usual skill; the fatal *échec* (check) was heard again and again, and a second time Napoleon was defeated.

The pieces were no sooner rearranged, than the emperor quietly removed a shawl from the shoulders of a lady near by, and with great care enveloped the face, neck, and body of the Turk, completing his arrangements with an exclamation of satisfaction. With a muffled nod the Moslem agreed to the new condition, and this third time, also, victory declared itself for the Turk. For a moment the emperor regarded his antagonist, then, with a gesture of scorn, he swept the Chess-men from the board, and crying "*Bagatelle!*" strode over knight and pawn, and so out of the room.—*The Chess Monthly, New York*.†

WHITE. Napoleon.	BLACK. Automaton.
1. P. to K.'s 4th.*	1. P. to K.'s 4th.
2. Q. to K. B.'s 3rd.	2. Q. Kt. to B.'s 3rd.
3. K. B. to Q. B.'s 4th.	3. K. Kt. to K. B.'s 3rd.
4. K. Kt. to K.'s 2nd.	4. K. B. to Q. B.'s 4th.
5. Q. R. P. to Q. R.'s 3rd.	5. P. to Q.'s 3rd.
6. Castles.	6. Q. B. to K. Kt.'s 5th.
7. Q. to Q.'s 3rd.	7. K. Kt. to K. R.'s 4th.
8. P. to K. R.'s 3rd.	8. B. takes Kt.
9. Q. takes B.	9. K. Kt. to K. B.'s 5th.
10. Q. to K.'s sq.	10. Q. Kt. to Q.'s 5th.
11. B. to Q. Kt.'s 3rd	11. K. Kt. takes K. R. P. (ch.)
12. K. to R.'s 2nd.	12. Q. to K. R.'s 5th.
13. P. to K. Kt.'s 3rd.	13. Q. Kt. to K. B.'s 6th (ch.)
14. K. to Kt.'s 2nd.	14. Kt. takes Q. (ch.)
15. R. takes Kt.	15. Q. to K. Kt.'s 5th.
16. P. to Q.'s 3rd.	16. B. takes K. B. P.
17. R. to K. R.'s sq.	17. Q. takes K. Kt. P. (ch.)
18. K. to K. B.'s sq.	18. B. to Q.'s 5th.
19. K. to K.'s 2nd.	

Black mated in four moves.

* For our "copy" of this game, we are indebted to Mr. W. Horner, of the Brooklyn Chess-club.

† "We cordially recommend the *Chess Monthly* to the patronage of American Chess-players.

C. D. MEAD, President of the New York Chess-club.

F. PERRIN, Secretary   "   "   "

T. FRÈRE, Secretary of the Brooklyn Chess-club."

TERMS. Annual subscription, Three Dollars, payable in advance. P. Miller & Son, publishers, No. 18 Thames-street, corner of Trinity-place, New York.

⁎ For the information of Chess-players who may visit New York, we would state, that besides the New York Club, which meets on Tuesday, Thursday, and Saturday evenings, at No. 19 E. Twelfth-street, players may always be found at the Union Chess Rooms, corner of Fulton and Nassau streets (Limberger's Saloon), every day from 10 A. M. until 3 P. M.

Endings of Games.

KING AND QUEEN AGAINST KING.

This is one of the simplest of all checkmates. It is only necessary to force the single king to the nearest side of the Chess-board, and then bringing up your own king, you mate in a very few moves. There is, however, one danger to be guarded against, viz., that of *stalemating* your adversary. The power of the queen being so great, renders you very liable to this error. Place your pieces as in Diagram 1, and find how to effect mate in two moves—observing the probability there is of your giving stalemate.

Diagram 1.

BLACK.

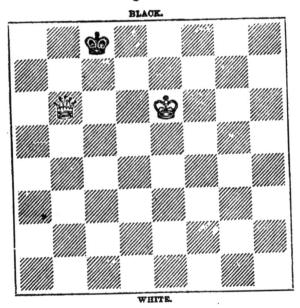

WHITE.

KING AND ROOK AGAINST KING.

This is also a very easy checkmate, though less so than the preceding one. A little practice, however, will enable you readily to master it. In fact, in the most favorable position for the single king, he cannot protract mate beyond eighteen or nineteen moves. As before, he must be

24*

driven to the side of the board, and then your king being placed in front of him, with one square between, mate is given by a check from the rook on the same side-line upon which the king stands. An example (see Diagram 2) will make this quite plain.

Diagram 2.

BLACK.

WHITE.

WHITE.	BLACK.
1. R. to K. R.'s 7th.	1. K. to K. B.'s sq.
2. K. to K.'s 2nd.	2. K. to K. Kt's sq.
3. R. to Q. R.'s 7th.	3. K. to K. B.'s sq.
4. K. to K.'s 3rd.	4. K. to K.'s sq.
5. K. to K.'s 4th.	5. K. to Q.'s sq.
6. K. to Q.'s 5th.	6. K. to Q. B.'s sq.
7. K. to Q.'s 6th.	7. K. to Q. Kt.'s sq.
8. R. to K. R.'s 7th.	

(8. R. to Q. B.'s 7th is still better, but the present move exhibits the principle more clearly.)

	8. K. to Q. B.'s sq.
9. R. to K. Kt.'s 7th.	9. K. to Q. Kt.'s sq.
10. K. to Q. B.'s 6th.	10. K. to R.'s sq.
11. K. to Q. Kt.'s 6th.	11. K. to Kt.'s sq.
12. R. to K. Kt.'s 8th (checkmate).	

In the following situation (see Diagram 3), examine how to give mate in three moves.

Diagram 8.

KING AND TWO BISHOPS AGAINST KING.

The two bishops also win, without much difficulty, against the king alone; but in this case the king must be forced, not only to a side of the board, but into one of the corners, or, at any rate, into a square adjoining a corner one. The following example (see Diagram 4) will be a sufficient illustration.

WHITE.	BLACK.
1. K. B. to K. R.'s 3rd.	1. K. to Q.'s sq.
2. Q. B. to K. B.'s 4th.	2. K. to K.'s 2nd.
3. K. to his 2nd.	3. K. to K. B.'s 3rd.
4. K. to K. B.'s 3rd.	4. K. to K.'s 2nd.
5. K. B. to K. B.'s 5th.	5. K. to K. B.'s 3rd.
6. K. to his Kt.'s 4th.	6. K. to his 2nd.
7. K. to his Kt.'s 5th.	7. K. to Q.'s sq.
8. K. to his B.'s 6th.	8. K. to K.'s sq.
9. Q. B. to Q. B.'s 7th.	9. K. to B.'s sq.
10. K. B. to Q.'s 7th.	10. K. to Kt.'s sq.
11. K. to his Kt.'s 6th.	11. K. to B.'s sq.
12. Q. B. to Q.'s 6th (ch.)	12. K. to Kt.'s sq.
13. K. B. to K.'s 6th (ch.)	13. K. to R.'s sq.
14. Q. B. checkmates.	

Diagram 4.

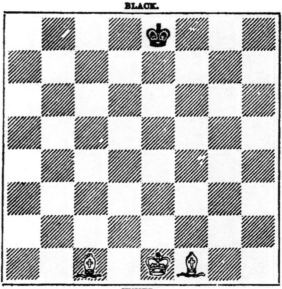

KING, BISHOP, AND KNIGHT AGAINST KING.

This is a much more difficult checkmate than any of the preceding ones, and should you be left with such a force at the termination of a game, you would probably find it quite impossible to win within the stipulated number of moves. This position merits a close examination, and you will then see that in this case the king must not only be driven into a corner of the board, but into one of them which is commanded by your bishop.

You will observe in this position (see Diagram 5) that the black king is in the most unfavorable situation for you, since he occupies a corner square which is not commanded by your bishop.

WHITE.	BLACK.
1. Kt. to K. B.'s 7th (ch.)	1. K. to Kt.'s sq.
2. B. to K.'s 4th.	2. K. to B.'s sq.
3. B. to K. R.'s 7th.	3. K. to his sq.
4. Kt. to K.'s 5th.	4. K. to his B.'s sq., or (A).
5. Kt. to Q.'s 7th (ch.)	5. K. to his sq.
6. K. to his 6th.	6. K. to Q.'s sq.
7. K. to Q.'s 6th.	7. K. to his sq. (best).
8. B. to K. Kt.'s 6th (ch.)	8. K. to Q.'s sq.

WHITE.	BLACK.
9. Kt. to Q. B.'s 5th.	9. K. to Q. B.'s sq.
10. K. B. to his 7th.	10. K. to Q.'s sq.
11. Kt. to Q. Kt.'s 7th (ch.)	11. K. to Q. B.'s sq.
12. K. to Q. B.'s 6th.	12. K. to Q. Kt.'s sq.
13. K. to Q. Kt.'s 6th.	13. K. to Q. B.'s sq.
14. B. to K.'s 6th (ch.)	14. K. to Q. Kt.'s sq.
15. Kt. to Q. B.'s 5th.	15. K. to Q. R.'s sq.
16. B. to Q.'s 7th.	16. K. to Q. Kt.'s sq
17. Kt. to Q. R.'s 6th (ch.)	17. K. to Q. R.'s sq.
18. B. to Q. B.'s 6th (checkmate).	

Diagram 5.

BLACK.

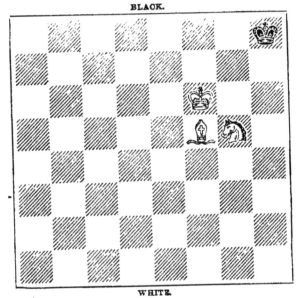

WHITE.

(A.)

	4. K. to Q.'s sq.
5. K. to his 6th.	5. K. to Q. B.'s 2nd.
6. Kt. to Q.'s 7th.	6. K. to Q. B.'s 3rd.

[This is his best move, to avoid the corner square; if, instead of this, he play his K. to Q. Kt.'s 2nd, your best move is the B. to Q.'s 3rd, and if he then play K. to Q. B.'s 3rd, you can move your B. to Q. B.'s 4th, and after his next move, B. to Q. Kt.'s 5th).

7. B. to Q.'s 3rd.	7. K. to Q. B.'s 2nd (best).
8. B. to Q. Kt.'s 5th.	8. K. to Q.'s sq.
9. Kt. to K.'s 5th.	9. K. to B.'s 2nd.
10. Kt. to Q. B.'s 4th.	10. K. to Q.'s square.
11. K. to Q.'s 6th.	11. K. to Q. B.'s sq.
12. Kt. to Q. R.'s 5th.	12. K. to Q.'s sq.
13. Kt. to Q. Kt.'s 7th (ch.)	13. K. to Q. B.'s sq.
14. K. to Q. B.'s 6th.	14. K. to Kt.'s sq.
15. Kt. to Q.'s 6th.	15. K. to R.'s 2nd.

16. K. to Q. B.'s 7th.	16. K. to R.'s sq.
17. B. to Q. B.'s 4th.	17. K. to R.'s 2nd.
18. Kt. to Q. B.'s 8th (ch.)	18. K. to R.'s sq.
19. B. to Q.'s 5th (checkmate).	

It not unfrequently happens, however, that when your opponent has a pawn besides the king, checkmate can be given without the necessity of driving him to the corner commanded by your bishop, because you do not then incur the risk of stalemating him.

KING AND TWO KNIGHTS AGAINST KING.

The two knights, with the assistance of the king, cannot force checkmate; unless, indeed, the adversary has a pawn, which may sometimes be made the means of effecting it with only a single knight, as will be seen hereafter. Many singular positions occur with the knights, where the adverse pawns, or even pieces, may be made to assist in crowding, and finally in checkmating their own monarch. The following is an example:

Diagram 6.

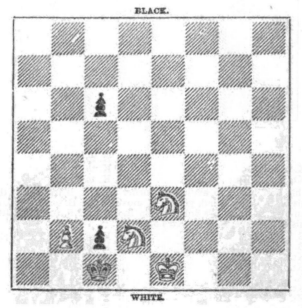

BLACK.

WHITE.

White mates in six moves, thus:

WHITE.	BLACK.
1. Kt. from K.'s 3rd to Q. B.'s 4th.	1. P. to Q. B.'s 4th.
2. P. to Q. Kt.'s 4th.	2. P. takes P.
3. K. to his 2nd.	3. P. to Q. Kt.'s 6th.
4. K. to his sq.	4. P. to Q. Kt.'s 7th.
5. Kt. to K's 5th.	5. P. Queens.
6. Kt. to Q.'s 3rd (checkmate).	

QUEEN AGAINST A KNIGHT OR BISHOP.

(In all cases, each party is of course understood to have a king in addition to the pieces named.)

The queen wins easily against one of the minor pieces, except when in such a position that the weaker party, by the sacrifice of the piece, may force a stalemate. As an example, see the following Diagram.

Diagram 7.

BLACK.

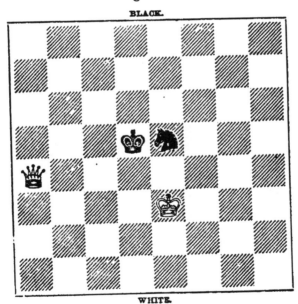

WHITE.

WHITE.	BLACK.
1. Q. to her 4th (ch.)	1. K. to his 3rd.
2. K. to his 4th.	

(If he move the Kt. to Q. B.'s 3rd, you should check with your Q. at her 5th, and then take the Kt.; but if he play—

WHITE.	BLACK.
	2. Kt. to K. Kt.'s 3rd.
8. Q. to her Kt.'s 6th (ch.)	3. K. to B.'s 2nd.
4. K. to B.'s 5th.	4. Kt. to K.'s 2nd (ch.)
5. K. to Kt.'s 5th.	5. Kt. to Q.'s 4th.
6. Q. to her 6th.	6. Kt. to K.'s 2nd.
7. Q. to K. B.'s 6th (ch.)	7. K. to his sq.
8. Q. to K.'s 6th.	8. K. to Q.'s sq.
9. K. to B.'s 6th.	9. Kt. to Q. B.'s sq.
10. Q. to Q. B.'s 6th.	

And you must win the Kt.

Whenever the knight is at a distance from the king, you may generally win it in a few moves by a divergent check, or by attacking and confining the knight; but you must always be careful to prevent your king and queen being attacked at the same time by the adverse knight; and to avoid positions in which black may draw by giving up his knight, as in the following Diagram, where, black having to move, can make a drawn game.

Diagram 8.

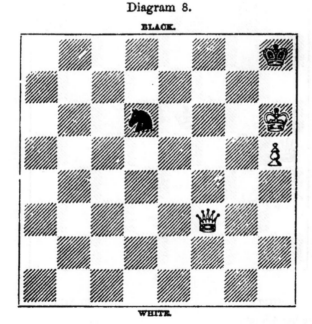

In the same manner, the queen easily wins against a bishop.

QUEEN AGAINST ROOK.

Here also, as in the last case, the queen wins in all general positions, the exceptions being of the same nature as before, viz., being founded on the possibility of making a stalemate.

Diagram 9.

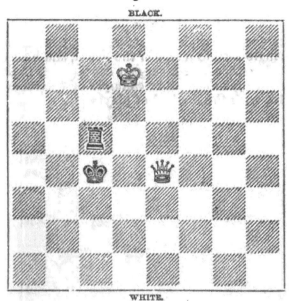

BLACK.

WHITE.

Philidor gives this position (Diagram 9), and the method of playing it. Black being already in check, he plays:

WHITE.	BLACK.
	1. K. to Kt.'s 6th.
2. K. to Q.'s 6th.	2. R. to Q. B.'s 7th.

(Should black play 2. R. to B.'s 5th, white's reply is 3. Q. to K.'s sq., and then to advance his king.)

3. K. to Q.'s 5th.	

(To check would be a loss of time.)

	3. K. to Kt.'s 7th.
4. K. to Q.'s 4th.	4. K. to R.'s 8th.

(Inviting white to take the rook, and thus give stalemate.)

5. K. to Q.'s 3rd.	5. R. to Kt.'s 7th.
6. Q. to K. R.'s 4th (ch.)	6. K. to Kt.'s 8th, or (A).
7. K. to B.'s 3rd.	7. R. to K. R.'s 7th.
8. Q. to Kt.'s 5th (ch.)	8. K. to R.'s 8th.
9. Q. to R.'s 6th (ch.)	9. K. to Kt.'s 8th.

WHITE.	BLACK.
10. Q. to Kt.'s 6th (ch.)	10. K. to R.'s 7th.
11. Q. to R.'s 7th (ch.)	11. K. to Kt.'s 8th.
12. Q. to Kt.'s 8th (ch.)	

Then takes rook, and wins.

(A.)

	6. R. to Q. R.'s 7th.
7. Q. to Q.'s sq. (ch.)	7. K. to Kt.'s 7th.
8. Q. to Q. B.'s 2nd (ch.)	8. K. to R.'s 6th.
9. Q. to Q. B.'s 3rd (ch.)	9. K. to R.'s 5th.
10. K. to Q. B.'s 4th.	

And wins.

With the exceptions already referred to, you can always force the single king to a side of the board, and afterwards win the rook, either by a divergent check, or as in the last variation. We give one other example of the same kind, Diagram 10, with the method of playing it.

Diagram 10.

BLACK.

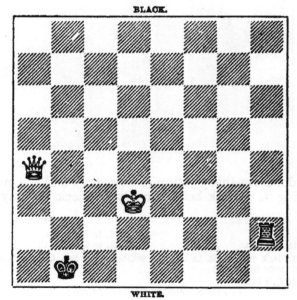

WHITE.

WHITE.	BLACK.
1. Q. to K. Kt.'s 4th.	

If he play R. to K. R.'s 2nd, white moves Q. to K. B.'s 5th; and if—

	1. R. to Q. B.'s 7th.
2. Q. to Q.'s sq. (ch.)	2. R. to Q. B.'s 8th.
3. Q. to Q. Kt.'s 3rd (ch.)	3. K. to R.'s 8th.
4. Q. to Q. R.'s 4th (ch.)	

(If, instead, you play K. to his 2nd, black moves R. to B.'s 7th (ch.), and will draw the game.)

5. K. to Q.'s 2nd.	4. K. to Kt.'s 7th.
6. Q. to Q. Kt.'s 5th (ch.)	5. R. to Q. Kt.'s 8th.
7. Q. to Q. R.'s 6th (ch.)	6. K. to R.'s 7th.
8. Q. to Q. R.'s 5th.	7. K. to Kt.'s 6th.
9. K. to Q.'s 3rd.	8. R. to Q. Kt.'s 7th (ch.)
10. Q. to Q. Kt.'s 5th (ch.)	9. R. to Q. Kt.'s 8th.
11. Q. to Q. R.'s 4th (ch.)	10. K. to R.'s 7th.
12. K. to Q.'s 2nd.	11. K. to Kt.'s 7th.

And wins.

Diagram 11.

BLACK.

WHITE.

In this position, Diagram 11, which is given by Ponziani, black, having the move, will draw the game.   Thus:

WHITE.	BLACK.
	1. R. to R.'s 2nd (ch.)
2. K. to Kt.'s 2nd.	2. R. to Kt.'s 2nd (ch.)
3. K. to B.'s 3rd.	3. R. to B.'s 2nd (ch.)
4. K. to Kt.'s 4th.	4. R. to Kt.'s 2nd (ch.)
5. K. to B.'s 5th.	5. R. to B.'s 2nd (ch.)
6. K. to Kt.'s 6th.	6. R. to Kt.'s 2nd (ch.)
7. K. to R.'s 6th.	7. R. to R.'s 2nd (ch.)

&c., for if white should take the rook, his adversary is stalemated.

KING AND PAWNS AGAINST KING AND PAWNS.

Diagram 12.   White can only draw.

WHITE.	BLACK.
1. P. two squares.	1. K. to B.'s sq.
2. K. to K.'s 7th.	2. P. two squares. (a)
8. K. to K.'s 6th.	8. K. to Q.'s sq.
4. K. takes P.	4. K. to Q.'s 2nd.

And draws.

(a) The only move to draw.

Diagram 12.

BLACK.

WHITE.

Diagram 18.   Black, with the move, cannot win.

WHITE.	BLACK.
	1. K. to K.'s 3rd.
2. K. to Q.'s 4th.	2. K. to Q.'s 2nd.
8. K. to Q.'s 5th.	8. K. to K.'s 2nd.
4. K. to Q. B.'s 4th.	4. K. to K.'s 3rd.
5. K. to Q.'s 4th.	

And draws.

White has only to wait for black to play to his king's third, and to answer either king to queen's fourth or king's bishop's fourth.

Diagram 13.

BLACK.

WHITE.

Diagram 14.

BLACK.

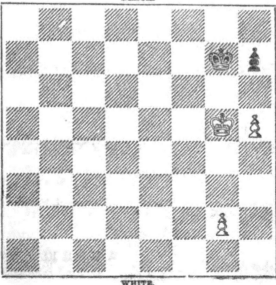

Diagram 14. White can only draw.

WHITE.	BLACK.
1. P. to K. Kt.'s 3rd	1. K. to K. R.'s sq.
2. K. to K. R.'s 6th.	2. K. to K. Kt.'s sq.
3. P. to K. Kt.'s 4th.	3. K. to K. R.'s sq.
4. P. to K. Kt.'s 5th.	4. K. to K. Kt.'s sq.
5. P. to K. Kt.'s 6th.	5. P. takes P.

And draws.

In order to save space, we omit the Diagrams in the endings of games, from this point, and give the positions, in type, instead.

BISHOPS AGAINST PAWN.
Position 15.

WHITE.	BLACK.
B. at Q. Kt.'s 7th.	P. at K. R.'s 5th.
B. at K.'s 7th.	K. at K. R.'s 6th.
K. at K. B.'s 4th.	

White to move and mate in four moves.

1. B. to Q. B.'s 5th.	Moves all forced.
2. K. to K. Kt.'s 4th.	
3. K. to K. B.'s 3rd.	
4. K. to K. Kt's 3rd.	

And mates.

Were black without a pawn, mate could not be effected so easily.

KNIGHT, BISHOP, AND PAWNS.
Position 16.

WHITE.	BLACK.
Kt. at K.'s 4th.	Pawns at K. B.'s 6th—K. Kt.'s 5th—
K. at K. R.'s 2nd.	and K. R.'s 6th.
	B. at K. Kt's 5th.
	K. at K. B.'s 8th.

White draws the game.

1. Kt. to K. B.'s 2nd.	1. P. one (ch.), or (A).
2. K. takes P.	2. P. to K. R.'s 7th, or (B).
3. K. takes P.	

And draws.

(A)
1. B. to K. R.'s 8th.

2. Kt. takes P. on K. Kt.'s 5th. (a)

And draws.

(B)
2. K. to K. Kt.'s 8th.

3. Kt. takes P. (ch.)

And draws.

(a) Had white in variation B taken the bishop with either king or knight, he would have lost.

This position at the first glance is likely to deceive even the veteran Chess-player.

ROOK AGAINST PAWNS.
Position 17.

WHITE.	BLACK.
Pawns at K. Kt.'s 6th and 7th.	R. at Q. R.'s 7th.
K. at K. B.'s 7th.	K. at Q. Kt.'s 2nd.

White wins, notwithstanding that black has the move.

	1. R. to K. B.'s 7th (ch.)
2. K. to K.'s 6th.	2. R. to K.'s 7th (ch.)
3. K. to K. B.'s 5th.	3. R. to K. B.'s 7th (ch.)
4. K. to K.'s 4th.	4. R. to K.'s 7th (ch.)
5. K. to K. B.'s 4th.	5. R. to K. sq. (best).
6. K. to K. Kt.'s 5th.	6. K. to Q. B.'s 2nd.
7. K. to K. R.'s 6th.	7. K. to Q.'s 2nd.
8. K. to K. R.'s 7th.	

And wins.

Had rook stood on Q. R.'s 2nd, or on any of the royal adverse squares, the game would have been drawn; but place the rook in any other position, and black must lose.

Position 18.

WHITE.	BLACK.
R. at K. Kt.'s sq.	Pawns at Q. R.'s 3rd—K.'s 7th—
K. at Q. B.'s 6th.	K. B.'s 6th—and K. R.'s 5th.

White, having the move, can draw against the four pawns.

1. K. to Q. B.'s 5th.	1. K. to Q. R.'s 5th.
2. K. to Q. B.'s 4th.	2. K. to Q. R.'s 6th (best).
3. K. to Q. B.'s 3rd.	3. K. to Q. R.'s 7th.
4. R. to K.'s sq.	4. P. to Q. R.'s 4th.
5. K. to Q.'s 3rd.	5. K. to Q. Kt.'s 7th.
6. K. to K.'s 3rd.	6. P. to Q. R.'s 5th.
7. K. takes P.	7. P. to Q. R.'s 6th.
8. R. takes P. (ch.)	

And draws.

This position exhibits the power of the rook, when well played, to stop the advance of pawns.

ROOK AGAINST BISHOP.
Position 19.

WHITE.	BLACK.
R. at K. Kt.'s 7th.	B. at K. B.'s 6th.
K. at K. B.'s 6th.	K. at K. B.'s sq.

White to move and win.

1. R. to K. Kt.'s 3rd.	1. B. to K.'s 5th.
2. R. to K. Kt.'s 4th.	2. B. to K. B.'s 6th.
3. R. to K. B.'s 4th.	3. B. to K. Kt.'s 7th, or (A)
4. R. to K. B.'s 2nd.	4. B. to Q. B.'s 3rd (best).
5. R. to Q. B.'s 2nd.	5. B. to Q.'s 2nd.
6. R. to Q. Kt.'s 2nd.	

And wins.

(A)

4. R. to K. B.'s 2nd.	3. B. to K.'s 7th.
• 5. R. to Q. B.'s 2nd.	4. B. to Q. B.'s 5th.
6. R. to Q. B.'s 6th.	5. B. to Q. R.'s 3rd.
7. R. to Q. Kt.'s 6th.	6. B. to Q. Kt.'s 2nd.

And wins.

(B)

7. R. to Q. B.'s 8th (ch.)	6. B. to Q. Kt.'s 4th.
8. R. to Q.'s 8th.	7. B. to K.'s sq.

And wins.

K. and R. against K. and B. generally draw, but in this instance the rook gives white the victory.

ROOK AGAINST ROOK AND PAWN.

Position 20.

WHITE.	BLACK.
R. at Q. R.'s sq.	R. at Q. R.'s sq.
K. at Q. B.'s 6th.	P. at Q. R.'s 3rd.
	K. at Q. Kt.'s sq.

White to move and win.

1. R. to K. R.'s sq.	1. K. to Q. R.'s 2nd. (a)
2. R. to K. R.'s 7th (ch.)	2. K. to Q. Kt.'s sq.
3. K. to Q. Kt.'s 6th.	

And wins.

(a) Any other move and white would mate with rook.

King and rook against king and rook generally draw, but in this instance black possesses a pawn, which costs him the game.

QUEEN AGAINST PAWNS.

Position 21.

WHITE.	BLACK.
Q. at K. R.'s 7th.	P. at K. Kt.'s 3rd.
K. at Q. R.'s sq.	K. at K. B.'s 4th.

White to move and win.

1. K. to Q. Kt.'s 2nd.	1. K. to K. B.'s 3rd.
2. K. to Q. B.'s 3rd.	2. P. one.
3. Q. to K.'s 4th. And wins.	

In the foregoing position white has only to advance his king, unless black pushes on the pawn.

Position 22.

WHITE.	BLACK.
Q. at Q. Kt.'s 7th.	P. at Q. B.'s 6th.
K. at K. Kt.'s 7th.	K. at Q. B.'s 8th.

White to move and win.

1. K. to K. B.'s 6th.	1. K. to Q.'s 8th.
2. K. to K.'s 5th.	2. P. one.
3. Q. to Q. Kt.'s 3rd.	3. K. to Q.'s 7th.
4. Q. to Q. R.'s 2nd.	4. K. to Q.'s 8th.
5. K. to Q.'s 4th.	5. K. to Q.'s 7th.
6. Q. to Q. Kt.'s 2nd.	6. K. to Q.'s 8th.
7. K. to Q.'s 3rd.	

And wins.

Had white king stood on king's knight's eighth, the same mode of play would be required as in Position 21. For example:

1. Q. to K. R.'s sq. (ch.)	1. K. to Q. Kt.'s 7th.
2. Q. to K. R.'s 8th.	2. K. to Q. Kt.'s 6th, or B.'s 7th.
3. Q. to Q.'s 4th.	

And wins.

Position 23.

WHITE.	BLACK.
Q. at K. B.'s 8th.	Pawns at K. B.'s 7th, and Q. Kt.'s 7th.
K. at Q. Kt.'s 8th.	K. at Q. R.'s 8th.

White to move and win.

1. Q. to Q. R.'s 3rd (ch.)	1. K. to Q. Kt.'s 8th.
2. Q. to Q. R.'s 6th.	2. K. to Q. B.'s 7th (best).
3. Q. to K.'s 2nd (ch.)	3. K. to Q. B.'s 6th.
4. Q. to K. B.'s sq.	

And wins.

QUEEN AGAINST ROOK.

Position 24.

WHITE.	BLACK.
Q. at K.'s sq.	R. at K. Kt.'s 2nd.
K. at K. B.'s 6th.	K. at K. R.'s sq.

White to move and win.

1. Q. to K. R.'s sq. (ch.)	1. K. to K. Kt.'s sq.
2. Q. to K. R.'s 5th.	2. R. to Q. B.'s 2nd (or A, B, C).
3. Q. to Q.'s 5th (ch.)	3. K. to K. R.'s 2nd.
4. Q. to Q.'s 3rd (ch.)	4. K. to K. Kt.'s sq.
5. Q. to Q.'s 8th.	

And wins.

(A)

3. Q. to K. Kt.'s 4th (ch.)	2. R. to Q. R.'s 2nd.
4. Q. to K. R.'s 4th (ch.)	3. K. to K. R.'s sq.
5. Q. to K. Kt.'s 3rd (ch.)	4. K. to K. Kt.'s sq.
6. Q. to K. R.'s 2nd (ch.)	5. K. to K. R.'s 2nd.
7. Q. to Q. Kt.'s 8th (ch.)	6. K. to K. Kt.'s sq.

And wins.

(B)

	2. R. to K. Kt.'s 6th.
3. Q. to K.'s 8th (ch.)	3. K. to K. R.'s 2nd.
4. Q. to K.'s 4th (ch.)	4. K. to K. Kt.'s sq.
5. Q. to Q. B.'s 4th (ch.)	5. K. to K. R.'s sq.
6. Q. to K. R.'s 4th (ch.)	

And wins.

(C)

	2. R. to K. Kt.'s 8th.
3. Q. to K.'s 8th (ch.)	3. K. to K. R.'s 2nd.
4. Q. to Q.'s 7th (ch.)	4. K. to K. R.'s sq. (best).
5. Q. to Q. B.'s 8th (ch.)	5. K. to K. R.'s 2nd.
6. Q. to Q. R.'s 7th (ch.)	6. K. to K. Kt.'s sq.
7. Q. to Q. Kt.'s 8th (ch.)	7. K. to K. R.'s 2nd.
8. Q. to K. R.'s 2nd (ch.)	

And wins.

King and queen win against king and rook, but it has not hitherto been shown with sufficient clearness how the rook may be won when separated from the king.

Position 25.

WHITE.	BLACK.
R. at Q. R.'s sq.	Q. at Q. Kt.'s 3rd.
K. at Q. R.'s 8th.	K. at Q.'s sq.

White has the move and draws.

1. R. to Q.'s sq. (ch.)	1. K. to Q. B.'s sq.
2. R. to Q. B.'s sq. (ch.)	2. K. to Q.'s sq.
3. R. to Q. B.'s 8th (ch.)	3. K. to Q.'s 2nd.
4. R. to Q. B.'s 7th (ch.)	4. K. to K.'s 3rd.
5. R. to K.'s 7th (ch.)	5. K. to Q.'s 4th.
6. R. to Q.'s 7th (ch.)	6. K. to Q. B.'s 5th.
7. R. to Q. B.'s 7th (ch.)	

And draws.

An exception to the rule laid down in the preceding illustration.

The Defeat of the Muzio Gambit.

GAME No. 1.

WHITE.	BLACK.
1. P. to K.'s 4th.	1. P. to K.'s 4th.
2. P. to K. B.'s 4th.	2. P. takes P.
8. Kt. to K. B.'s 3rd.	8. P. to K. Kt.'s 4th.
4. B. to Q. B.'s 4th.	4. P. to K. Kt.'s 5th.
5. Castles.	5. Q. to K.'s 2nd.
6. P. to Q.'s 4th.	6. P. takes Kt.
7. Kt. to Q. B.'s 3rd.	7. P. to Q.'s 3rd. (a)
8. Kt. to Q.'s 5th.	8. Q. to Q.'s 2nd.
9. Q. takes P.	9. Kt. to Q. B.'s 3rd.
10. P. to K.'s 5th.	10. P. takes P.
11. P. takes P. (or A, B). (b)	11. Kt. to Q.'s 5th.
12. Q. to K. R.'s 5th. (c)	12. Kt. to K.'s 3rd.
18. B. takes P. (or C).	18. P. to Q. B.'s 3rd.
14. Kt. to K.'s 3rd (best).	14. Kt. to K. Kt.'s 2nd.
15. Q. to K. Kt.'s 5th (or D).	15. Q. to K.'s 2nd.
16. Q. to K. Kt.'s 3rd.	16. Kt. to K. R.'s 4th.
17. Q. to K. B.'s 3rd.	17. Kt. takes B.
18. Q. takes Kt.	18. B. to K.'s 3rd.

And black has a winning game.

(A)

11. Q. to K. R.'s 5th.	11. K. to Q.'s sq.
12. Q. to K. Kt.'s 5th (ch.) (d)	12. P. to K. B.'s 3rd.
18. Kt. takes K. B. P.	18. Q. to K. Kt.'s 2nd.
14. Q. takes Q.	14. B. takes Q.
15. Kt. takes Kt. (e)	15. Kt. takes P.
16. R. to Q.'s sq. (f)	16. K. to K.'s sq.
17. P. to Q. B.'s 3rd.	17. Q. B. to K.'s 3rd.

And black wins easily.

(B)

11. R. to K.'s sq.	11. K. to Q.'s sq.
12. P. takes P.	12. Q. to K. Kt.'s 5th.
18. Q. to Q.'s 3rd.	18. B. to K. B.'s 4th.
14. Q. to Q.'s 2nd.	14. B. to Q. B.'s 4th (ch.)
15. K. to R.'s sq.	15. K. to Q. B.'s sq.

And black wins.

(C)

18. R. to Q.'s sq.	18. Q. to Q. B.'s 3rd.
14. B. to Q. Kt.'s 3rd.	14. B. to Q.'s 2nd.
15. Kt. takes P. on K. B.'s 5th.	15. Castles.
16. Q. takes K. B. P.	16. Kt. to K. R.'s 3rd.

And black wins.

(D)

15. Q. to K. R.'s 4th. (g)	15. B. to K.'s 2nd.
16. B. to K. Kt.'s 5th.	16. Kt. to K.'s 3rd.
17. B. takes B.	17. Q. takes B.

And black wins.

(a) P. to Q. B.'s 3rd would be weak play.

(b) If white play Q. to K.'s 4th, black's answer is K. to Q.'s square, and would have a winning game.

(c) Were white to take P. on K. B.'s 5th, black would take Kt. with Q., and win easily.

(d) Q. to R.'s 4th (ch.) would be inferior play.

(e) If Q. P. were to take P., black Kt. would take P.; and if B. were to check, black would interpose with bishop, and win easily.

(f) Any other mode of play cannot prevent black from regaining his lost piece.

(g) White queen is compelled to retire from rook's 5th, and white cannot now play his rook to queen's square with advantage.

GAME No. 2.

WHITE.	BLACK.
1. P. to K.'s 4th.	1. P. to K.'s 4th.
2. P. to K. B.'s 4th.	2. P. takes P.
3. Kt. to K. B.'s 3rd.	3. P. to K. Kt.'s 4th.
4. B. to Q. B.'s 4th.	4. P. to K. Kt.'s 5th.
5. P. to Q.'s 4th.	5. P. takes Kt.
6. Q. takes P. (or A).	6. Q. to K.'s 2nd. (a)
7. Q. takes P. (or B, C).	7. Kt. to Q. B.'s 3rd.
8. Castles.	8. Kt. to Q.'s sq.
9. Kt. to Q. B.'s 3rd. (b)	9. P. to Q.'s 3rd.
10. Kt. to Q.'s 5th.	10. Q. to Q.'s 2nd.

And the position becomes the same as though black had castled at the 5th move.

(A)

6. Castles.	6. Q. to K.'s 2nd.
7. Q. takes P.	7. Kt. to Q. B.'s 3rd.
8. B. takes P. on K. B.'s 5th.	8. P. to Q.'s 3rd.
9. B. to K. Kt.'s 5th.	9. P. to K. B.'s 3rd.
10. Q. to R.'s 5th (ch.)	10. K. to Q.'s sq.
11. B. takes K. Kt.	11. P. takes Q. B.
12. R. to K. B.'s 7th.	12. Q. to K.'s sq.
13. Q. takes P. (ch.) (or D).	13. Kt. to K.'s 2nd.

And black wins.

(B)

7. Kt. to Q. B.'s 3rd.	7. P. to Q.'s 3rd.
8. P. to K.'s 5th.	8. Kt. to Q. B.'s 3rd.
9. Kt. to Q.'s 5th.	9. Q. to Q.'s 2nd.
10. Q. takes P. on K. B.'s 5th.	10. P. takes P.
11. P. takes P.	11. Kt. to Q.'s sq.
12. Castles.	12. P. to Q. B.'s 3rd.
13. Kt. to K. B.'s 6th (ch.)	13. Kt. takes Kt.
14. Q. takes Kt. (c)	14. R. to K. Kt.'s sq.
15. Q. B. to K. Kt.'s 5th.	15. Q. to K.'s 2nd.

And black wins.

(C)

7. P. to K.'s 5th.	7. Kt. to Q. B.'s 3rd.
8. Q. takes K. P. on K. B.'s 5th (or E, F).	8. B. to K. R.'s 3rd.
9. Q. to K. Kt.'s 3rd.	9. B. takes Q. B.
10. Q. to K. Kt.'s 7th.	10. Q. to K. B.'s sq.
11. Q. takes R.	11. B. takes Q. Kt. P.
12. R. to K. B.'s sq.	12. Kt. to K. R.'s 3rd.

And black wins.

(D)

13 B. takes R. P.	13. Kt. to K.'s 2nd.
14. P. to Q.'s 5th.	14. B. to K. Kt.'s 2nd. (*d*)

And black wins.

(E)

8. Q. to K.'s 4th.	8. Kt. to K. B.'s 3rd. (*e*)
9. Q. takes P. on K. B.'s 5th (or G).	9. P. to Q.'s 4th.
10. B. to Q. Kt.'s 3rd.	10. Kt. to K. Kt.'s 5th.

And black wins.

(F)

8. P. to Q. B.'s 3rd.	8. P. to Q.'s 3rd.
9. Castles.	9. P. takes P.
10. B. to Q. Kt.'s 5th.	10. B. to Q.'s 2nd.

And black wins.

(G)

9. Q. to K.'s 2nd.	9. Kt. takes Q. P.
10. Q. to her 3rd sq. (*f*)	10. P. to Q.'s 4th.

And black wins.

(*a*) Q. to K.'s 2nd, with the assistance of Q. Kt., will always be able to defend the king's side, let white play as he may.

(*b*) If queen were to take Q. B. P., black would play his queen to her 3rd, and win easily.

(*c*) If white were to take knight with pawn instead of queen, black would answer queen to her 3rd.

(*d*) The decisive move.

(*e*) This move completely frustrates white's attack.

(*f*) White might take Kt. with P., the moves would then follow as under:

10.	10. Q. takes Q. (ch.)
11. B. takes Q.	11. Kt. takes Q. B. P. (ch.)

And black wins.

GAME No. 3.*

WHITE.	BLACK.
1. P. to K.'s 4th.	1. P. to K.'s 4th.
2. P. to K. B.'s 4th.	2. P. takes P.
3. Kt. to K. B.'s 3rd.	3. P. to K. Kt.'s 4th.
4. B. to Q. B.'s 4th.	4. P. to K. Kt.'s 5th.
5. Castles.	5. Q. to Q.'s 2nd.
6. Kt. to K.'s 5th (or A, B).	6. Q. takes Kt.
7. P. to Q.'s 4th.	7. Q. to K. Kt.'s 2nd.
8. R. takes P. (or C).	8. Kt. to K. R.'s 3rd.

* This and the following games, although exhibiting fine play, are not so strong, either in attack or defence, as the two preceding examples.

9. R. to K. B.'s sq.	9. P. to Q.'s 3rd. (a)
10. B. takes Kt.	10. Q. takes B.
11. B. takes P. (ch.)	11. K. to Q.'s sq.
12. P. to K.'s 5th.	12. Kt. to Q. B.'s 3rd.

And black wins.

(A)

6. Kt. to Q.'s 4th.	6. Q. to Q. B.'s 4th.
7. P. to Q. B.'s 3rd.	7. Q. takes B.
8. Q. takes P. on K. Kt.'s 5th.	8. Kt. to Q. B.'s 3rd.
9. Q. takes P. on K. B.'s 5th.	9. P. to K. B.'s 3rd.
10. P. to Q. Kt.'s 3rd.	10. Kt. takes Kt.

And black wins.

(B)

6. P. to Q.'s 4th.	6. P. takes Kt.
7. Q. takes P.	7. P. to Q.'s 3rd.
8. Q. B. takes P.	8. B. to K.'s 3rd.
9. P. to K.'s 5th.	9. P. to Q.'s 4th.
10. B. takes P.	10. B. takes B.
11. Q. takes B.	11. Kt. to Q. B.'s 3rd.

And black has the better game.

(C)

8. Q. B. takes P.	8. P. to Q.'s 3rd.
9. B. takes P. (ch.)	9. K. to Q.'s sq.
10. P. to K.'s 5th.	10. Kt. to Q. B.'s 3rd.

And black has the better game.

(a) Black might also play P. to K. B.'s 3rd, and have the better game.

GAME No. 4.

WHITE.	BLACK.
1. P. to K.'s 4th.	1. P. to K.'s 4th.
2. P. to K. B.'s 4th.	2. P. takes P.
3. Kt. to K. B.'s 3rd.	3. P. to K. Kt.'s 4th.
4. B. to Q. B.'s 4th.	4. P. to K. Kt.'s 5th.
5. Castles.	5. Q. to K.'s 2nd.
6. P. to Q.'s 4th.	6. P. takes Kt.
7. Q. takes P.	7. Kt. to Q. B.'s 3rd.
8. Kt. to Q. B.'s 3rd.	8. P. to Q.'s 3rd.
9. Kt. to Q.'s 5th.	9. Q. to Q.'s 2nd.
10. Q. takes P.	10. Kt. to Q.'s sq.
11. P. to K.'s 5th.	11. Kt. to K.'s 3rd.
12. Kt. to K. B.'s 6th (ch.)	12. Kt. takes Kt.
13. Q. takes Kt.	13. R. to K. Kt.'s sq.
14. P. to Q.'s 5th.	14. Kt. to Q.'s sq.
15. P. to K.'s 6th (or A, B).	15. P. takes P.
16. P. takes P.	16. Kt. takes P.

And black has a winning game.

(A)

15. P. takes P.	15. Q. takes P.
16. R. to K.'s sq. (ch.)	16. B. to K.'s 2nd.
17. B. to K. Kt.'s 5th.	17. R. takes B.
18. Q. takes R. (or C).	18. K. to K. B.'s sq.

And black wins.

(B)

15. R. to K.'s sq.	15. Q. to K.'s 2nd.
16. Q. to K. B.'s 4th.	16. R. to K. Kt.'s 6th.
17. Q. to K. B.'s sq.	17. P. takes P.

And black wins.

(C)

18. Q. to K. R.'s 8th (ch.)	18. K. to Q.'s 2nd.
19. B. to Q. Kt.'s 5th (ch.)	19. P. to Q. B.'s 3rd.
20. P. takes P. (ch.)	20. P. takes P.
21. Q. R. to Q.'s sq.	21. R. to Q.'s 4th.
22. B. to K.'s 2nd.	22. K. to Q. B.'s 2nd.

And black wins.

GAME No. 5.

WHITE.	BLACK.
1. P. to K.'s 4th.	1. P. to K.'s 4th.
2. P. to K. B.'s 4th.	2. P. takes P.
3. Kt. to K. B.'s 3rd.	3. P. to K. Kt.'s 4th.
4. B. to Q. B.'s 4th.	4. P. to K. Kt.'s 5th.
5. Castles.	5. Q. to K.'s 2nd.
6. P. to Q.'s 4th.	6. P. takes Kt.
7. Q. Kt. to B.'s 3rd.	7. P. to Q.'s 3rd.
8. Kt. to Q.'s 5th.	8. Q. to Q.'s 2nd.
9. Q. takes P.	9. Kt. to Q. B.'s 3rd.
10. P. to K.'s 5th.	10. Kt. takes Q. P.
11. Q. to K.'s 4th.	11. Kt. to K.'s 3rd.
12. Kt. takes P. on K. B.'s 5th.	12. P. takes P.
13. Kt. takes Kt.	13. P. takes Kt.
14. Q. takes P. on K.'s 4th.	14. Q. to K. Kt.'s 2nd.
15. R. takes B. (ch.)	15. K. takes R.
16. B. to K. B.'s 4th.	16. Kt. to K. B.'s 3rd (or A).
17. R. to K. B.'s sq.	17. K. to K.'s sq.
18. B. to K. R.'s 6th.	18. Q. takes B.
19. R. takes Kt.	

And white has the better game.

(A)

16.	16. Q. takes Q.
17. B. takes Q.	17. Kt. to K. B.'s 3rd.
18. B. takes Kt.	18. R. to K. Kt.'s sq.
19. B. to Q.'s 3rd.	19. P. to K. R.'s 3rd (best).
20. R. to K. B.'s sq.	20. K. to K.'s sq.
21. B. to K.'s 5th.	21. P. to Q. B.'s 3rd.
22. R. to K. B.'s 6th.	22. R. to K. R.'s sq.
23. R. to K. B.'s 4th.	23. R. to K. B.'s sq.
24. R. to K. R.'s 4th.	

And white has the better game.

GAME No. 6.

WHITE.	BLACK.
1. P. to K.'s 4th.	1. P. to K.'s 4th.
2. P. to K. B.'s 4th.	2. P. takes P.
3. K. Kt. to B.'s 3rd.	3. P. to K. Kt.'s 4th.
4. B. to Q. B.'s 4th.	4. P. to K. Kt.'s 5th.

5. Castles.	5. Q. to K.'s 2nd.
6. P. to Q.'s 4th.	6. P. takes Kt.
7. Q. takes P.	7. P. to Q.'s 3rd.
8. B. takes P. on K. Kt.'s 5th.	8. B. to K.'s 3rd.
9. P. to K.'s 5th (or A).	9. B. takes B.
10. Q. takes Q. Kt. P.	10. B. takes R.
11. Q. takes R.	11. Q. to Q.'s sq.
12. K. takes B.	12. P. to Q. R.'s 3rd.

And black has a winning game.

(A

9. B. to K. Kt.'s 5th.	9. Q. takes B.
10. B. takes B.	10. Kt. to K. R.'s 3rd.
11. Q. to Q. Kt.'s 3rd.	11. P. takes B.
12. Q. takes Kt. P.	12. Q. to K.'s 6th (ch.)
13. K. to R.'s sq.	13. Q. takes Q. P.
14. Q. takes R.	14. Q. to Q. Kt.'s 3rd.
15. Kt. to Q. B.'s 3rd.	15. K. to K.'s 2nd.

And black has the better game.

GAME No. 7.

WHITE.	BLACK.
1. P. to K.'s 4th.	1. P. to K.'s 4th.
2. P. to K. B.'s 4th.	2. P. takes P.
3. Kt. to K. B.'s 3rd.	3. P. to K. Kt.'s 4th.
4. B. to Q. B.'s 4th.	4. P. to K. Kt.'s 5th.
5. Castles.	5. Q. to K.'s 2nd.
6. P. to Q.'s 4th.	6. P. takes Kt.
7. Kt. to Q. B.'s 3rd.	7. P. to Q.'s 3rd.
8. Kt. to Q.'s 5th.	8. Q. to Q.'s 2nd.
9. Q. takes P.	9. Kt. to Q. B.'s 3rd.
10. P. to K.'s 5th.	10. P. takes P.
11. Q. to K.'s 4th.	11. K. to Q.'s sq.
12. P. takes P.	12. B. to Q. B.'s 4th (ch.)
13. K. moves.	13. Q. to K. B.'s 4th.
14. Q. to K.'s 2nd.	14. Q. takes P. on K.'s 4th.
15. Q. takes Q.	15. Kt. takes Q.

And black wins.

GAME No. 8.

WHITE.	BLACK.
1. P. to K.'s 4th.	1. P. to K.'s 4th.
2. P. to K. B.'s 4th.	2. P. takes P.
3. K. Kt. to B.'s 3rd.	3. P. to K. Kt.'s 4th.
4. K. B. to Q. B.'s 4th.	4. P. to K. Kt.'s 5th.
5. Castles.	5. Q. to K.'s 2nd.
6. P. to Q.'s 4th.	6. P. takes Kt.
7. Q. takes P.	7. P. to Q.'s 3rd.
8. Q. takes P.	8. Q. B. to K.'s 3rd.
9. P. to Q.'s 5th.	9. B. to Q.'s 2nd.
10. P. to K.'s 5th.	10. P. takes P.
11. Q. to K. B.'s 2nd.	11. P. to K. B.'s 3rd.
12. Kt. to Q. B.'s 3rd.	12. Q. to Q. B.'s 4th.

And black wins.

GAME No. 9.

WHITE.	BLACK.
1. P. to K.'s 4th.	1. P. to K.'s 4th.
2. P. to K. B.'s 4th.	2. P. takes P.
3. Kt. to K. B.'s 3rd.	3. P. to K. Kt.'s 4th.
4. B. to Q. B.'s 4th.	4. P. to K. Kt.'s 5th.
5. P. to Q.'s 4th.	5. P. takes Kt.
6. Q. takes P.	6. Kt. to Q. B.'s 3rd.
7. Q. B. takes P.	7. Q. to K.'s 2nd.
8. Q. B. takes P.	8. P. to Q.'s 3rd.
9. Q. B. takes P.	9. Q. takes B.
9. Q. takes B. P. (ch.)	10. K. to Q.'s sq.
1. Castles.	11. Kt. to K. R.'s 3rd.

And black wins.

Chess Problems.

PROBLEM No. 1.—BY D. JULLIEN.

White to play, and checkmate in two moves.

BLACK.

WHITE.

26*

PROBLEM No. 6.—BY EUGENE B. COOK.

White to play, and checkmate in four moves.

BLACK.

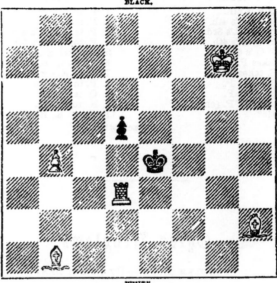

WHITE.

PROBLEM No. 7.—BY S. LOYD.

White to play, and checkmate in four moves.

BLACK.

WHITE.

PROBLEM NO. 8.—BY I. S. LOYD, JR.
White to play, and checkmate in four moves.

PROBLEM NO. 9.—BY EUGENE B. COOK.
White to play, and checkmate in four moves.

PROBLEM No. 10.—BY D. JULLIEN.

White to play, and checkmate in five moves.

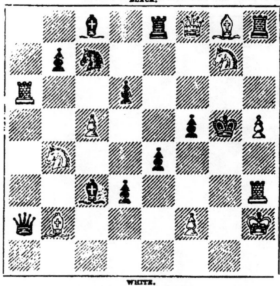

PROBLEM No. 11.—BY PROF. A. CLAPP.

White to play, and checkmate in five moves.

PROBLEM No. 12.—BY EUGENE B. COOK.
White to play, and checkmate in five moves.

BLACK.

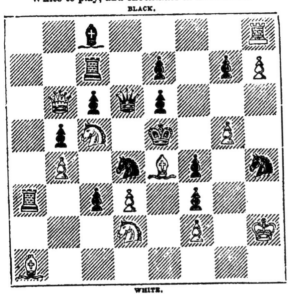

WHITE.

PROBLEM No. 13.—BY N. MARACHE.
White to play, and checkmate in five moves.

BLACK.

WHITE.

PROBLEM No. 14.—"THE JESUIT." BY EUGENE B. COOK.

White to play, and checkmate in nine moves.

PROBLEM No. 15.—SELF-MATE. BY EUGENE B. COOK.

White to play, and force black to checkmate him (white) in seven moves.

PROBLEM No. 16.—"THE CIRCUS." BY EUGENE B. COOK.
White to play and draw the game.

PROBLEM No. 17.—ANONYMOUS.

WHITE.—Q. at K.'s 4th; R. at Q. R.'s sq.; R. at K. R.'s 8th; K. at K. B.'s 6th.
BLACK.—R. at Q. R.'s 2nd; R. at Q. Kt.'s sq.; P. at Q. Kt.'s 2nd; K. at Q. R.'s sq.

White to play, and checkmate in two moves.

PROBLEM No. 18.—BY STANLEY.

WHITE.—P. at Q. Kt.'s 2nd; R. at K.'s 2nd; B. at K. Kt.'s 2nd; Kt. at K. B.'s 5th; K. at Q.'s sq.
BLACK.—B. at Q. Kt.'s 2nd; K. at Q.'s 6th.

White to play, and checkmate in two moves. .

PROBLEM No. 19.—BY HORWITZ.

WHITE.—P. at K.'s 5th; Q. at Q. R.'s 6th; Kt. at K. Kt.'s 6th; K. at Q. B.'s 3rd.
BLACK.—K. at Q. B.'s 4th.

White to play, and checkmate in three moves.

PROBLEM No. 20.—THE INDIAN PROBLEM.

WHITE.—Pawns at Q. Kt.'s 2nd, K. B.'s 2nd, and K. Kt.'s 4th; R. at Q.'s sq.; B. at K. Kt.'s 2nd; B. at K. R.'s 6th; K. at Q. R.'s sq.
BLACK.—Pawns at K.'s 4th and Q. Kt.'s 2nd; Kt. at K. B.'s 6th; K. at K.'s 5th.

White to play, and checkmate in four moves.

PROBLEM No. 21.—BY HERR KLING.

WHITE.—Pawns at Q.'s 2nd and K.'s 4th; R. at Q. R.'s 6th; B. at K. R.'s 8th; K. at K.'s 2nd.
BLACK.—Pawns at Q.'s 2nd, K. R.'s 2nd, and K. R.'s 6th; K. at K. R.'s 7th.

White to play, and checkmate in four moves.

PROBLEM No. 22.—BY HERR HARRWITZ.

WHITE.—Pawns at Q. Kt.'s 2nd, K. B.'s 2nd, K. Kt.'s 3rd. and K. R.'s 5th; R. at Q. R.'s 3rd; B. at Q. R.'s 6th; Kt. at K. B.'s sq.; Kt. at K. Kt.'s sq.; K. at Q. R.'s sq.
BLACK.—Pawns at Q. B.'s 3rd, K. B.'s 3rd, and K.'s 5th; Q. at Q. B.'s 4th; B. at K.'s 4th; B. at Q.'s 6th; Kt. at Q.'s 4th; K. at Q.'s 5th.

White to play, and checkmate in four moves.

PROBLEM No. 23.—BY D. JULLIEN.

WHITE.—Pawns at Q. B.'s 3rd and Q. Kt.'s 4th; R. at K.'s 5th; B. at Q.'s sq.; Kt. at K.'s 4th; K. at K. B.'s 4th.
BLACK.—P. at Q.'s 2nd; K. at Q. B.'s 5th.

White to play, and checkmate in four moves.

PROBLEM No. 24.—BY N. MARACHE.

WHITE.—P. at Q. Kt.'s 5th; Q. at Q. Kt.'s 7th; Rooks at K. R.'s 3rd and 7th; B. at K. Kt.'s sq.; Kt. at Q.'s 3rd; K. at Q. R.'s 4th.
BLACK.—Pawns at Q.'s 3rd, Q. B.'s 4th, and Q.'s 7th; Q. at Q.'s 2nd; Rooks at Q. Kt.'s 6th and 7th; B. at Q. B.'s sq.; B. at K. Kt.'s 2nd; K. at Q. B.'s 6th.

White to play, and checkmate in four moves.

PROBLEM No. 25.—BY EUGENE B. COOK.

WHITE.—P. at Q. B.'s 4th; B. at Q. B.'s 7th; B. at Q.'s 5th; Kt. at K. R.'s sq.; K. at R.'s 5th.
BLACK.—Pawns at K. B.'s 3rd and K. R.'s 2nd; Kt. at K.'s 5th; K. at K. B.'s 4th.

White to play, and checkmate in five moves.

PROBLEM No. 26.—BY T. M. BROWN.

WHITE.—Pawns at K. Kt.'s 4th and K. R.'s 2nd; R. at K. B.'s 8th; Bishops at Q. Kt.'s 5th and K. Kt.'s 3rd; K. at Q. B.'s 4th.
BLACK.—P. at K. Kt.'s 3rd; K. at K.'s 5th.

White to play, and checkmate in six moves.

PROBLEM No. 27.—BY EUGENE B. COOK.

WHITE.—Pawns at Q.'s 3rd and K. R.'s 4th; R. at K.'s 3rd; B. at Q. R.'s 7th; B. at K. R.'s 3rd; K. at Q. R.'s sq.
BLACK.—Pawns at K. R.'s 2nd and 3rd; K. at K. B.'s 5th.

White to play, and checkmate in five moves.

PROBLEM No. 28.—BY I. S. LOYD, JR.

WHITE.—Pawns at Q.'s 2nd, Q. B.'s 5th, K.'s 3rd, K. Kt.'s 3rd, K. R.'s 3rd, and K. R.'s 4th; Q. at Q. B.'s 4th; B. at K. B.'s 6th; Kt. at Q. B.'s 5th; Kt. at K. B.'s 4th; K. at K. R.'s 7th.
BLACK.—Pawns at Q. B.'s 3rd, K. B.'s 2nd, and K. B.'s 6th; Rooks at Q. B.'s 2nd and Q.'s 6th; Knights at K.'s 2nd and Q. B.'s 8th; Q. at Q. Kt.'s 4th; B. at Q.'s 4th; K. at K. B.'s 4th.

White to play, and checkmate in five moves.

PROBLEM No. 29.—BY EUGENE B. COOK.

WHITE.—Kt. at Q. Kt.'s 7th; B. at Q. B.'s 4th; Kt. at K.'s 3rd; K. at K. Kt.'s 4th.

BLACK.—Pawn at K.'s 4th B at Q.'s 3rd; K. at K.'s 5th.

White to play, and checkmate in six moves.

PROBLEM No. 30.—BY T. M. BROWN.

WHITE.—P. at Q.'s 3rd; Q. at Q. R.'s 6th; Kt. at Q. B.'s 8th; R. at K.'s 8th; R. at K. R.'s 4th; B. at K. R.'s 3rd; K. at Q. Kt.'s 7th.

BLACK.—Pawns at Q. B.'s 2nd. 4th, 5th, Q.'s 2nd, 3rd. 5th, and K. B.'s 2nd, 4th (eight pawns); Bishops at Q.'s sq. and K.'s 5th; Q. at K. R.'s 7th; Kt. at Q. Kt.'s 4th; K. at Q.'s 4th.

White to play, and checkmate in eight moves, without taking any of Black's pawns.

PROBLEM No. 31.—BY HERR KLING.

WHITE.—All the pieces on their own squares, but no pawns on the board.

BLACK.—King at his square.

White playing first, undertakes to command every square on the board in fourteen moves, mating only at the last move.

SOLUTIONS TO THE CHESS PROBLEMS.

PROBLEM No. 1.

WHITE.	BLACK.
1. R. takes B. (ch.)	1. K. takes R. (dis. ch.)
2. Q. interposes (checkmate).	

PROBLEM No. 2.

WHITE.	BLACK.
1. Q. to K. R.'s 6th.	1. B. takes Q.
2. B. takes P.	2. B. moves.
3. B. takes P. (checkmate).	
	1. P. takes Q.
2. B. takes P. (ch.)	2. B. to B.'s 3rd.
3. B. takes B. (checkmate).	
	1. B. to B.'s 3rd.
2 B. to K.'s 7th.	2. Any move.
3 Mates.	

PROBLEM No. 3.

WHITE.	BLACK.
1. R. to R.'s 3rd (dis. ch.)	1. Moves.
2. B. to R.'s 6th.	2. Moves.
3. B. to B.'s 8th (checkmate).	

PROBLEM No. 4.

WHITE.	BLACK.
1. Q. to Kt.'s 7th (ch.)	1. B. takes Q.
2. P. takes B.	2. B. moves.
3. B. takes B. (checkmate).	

PROBLEM No. 5.

WHITE.
1. Kt. takes Q. B.'s P. (dis. ch.)
2. R. to Q.'s 5th (double ch.)
3. Kt. to K.'s 3rd (ch.)
4. P. checkmates.

BLACK.
1. Q. takes Q.
2. K. takes R.
3. R. takes Kt.

PROBLEM No. 6.

WHITE.
1. R. to Q. R.'s 3rd (ch.)
2. K. to K. B.'s 6th.
3. B. to Q.'s 3rd (ch.)
4. B. to Q.'s 6th (checkmate).

4. B. to Q. Kt.'s 6th (checkmate).

BLACK.
1. K. to Q.'s 5th.
2. K. to B.'s 5th.
3. K. takes P.

3. K. to Q.'s 5th.

PROBLEM No. 7.

WHITE.
1. Q. to R.'s 6th (ch.)
2. R. to R.'s sq. (ch.)
3. Kt. to R.'s 3rd.
4. Kt. or R. (checkmate.)

BLACK.
1. P. takes Q.
2. R. to R.'s 5th.
3. Moves.

PROBLEM No. 8.

WHITE.
1. R. takes P. (ch.)
2. B. to K.'s 5th.
3. R. to Q.'s 8th (ch.)
4. K. to B.'s 7th (checkmate).

BLACK.
1. K. to B.'s 2nd.
2. Q. takes Kt. (ch.)
3. K. takes R.

PROBLEM No. 9.

WHITE.
1. K. to K.'s 2nd.
2. K. to K. B.'s 3rd.
3. K. to K.'s 3rd.
4. B. to K. B.'s 4th (checkmate).

2. K. to B.'s 3rd.
3. Q. takes B.
4. B. to B.'s 4th (checkmate).

2. K. to K.'s 3rd.
3. P. to B.'s 4th (ch.)
4. Q. takes P. (checkmate).

2. B. to B.'s 4th (ch.)
3. Q. to Q. 2nd (ch.)
4. Q. to Q.'s 6th (checkmate).

BLACK.
1. R. takes Q. (ch.)
2. B. to K.'s 7th (ch.)
3. Anywhere.

1. R. to Kt.'s 5th (ch.)
2. B. to K.'s 7th (ch.) (best).
3. R. takes Kt.

1. R. to Kt.'s 2nd (ch.)
2. R. takes Kt.
3. K. takes B.

1. P. to K. Kt.'s 7th, or R. takes R.
2. K. takes B.
3. K. to K.'s 4th.

PROBLEM No. 10.

WHITE.
1. Q. takes Q.'s P.
2. R. interposes (ch.)
3. R.'s P. 1.
4. Q. R. to R.'s 4th.
5. Kt. or Q. (checkmate).

BLACK.
1. B. checks (best).
2. K. to K. B.'s 5th (best).
3. Q. to K. B.'s 2nd. (A)
4. Any thing.

(A)

4. P. takes R. (ch.)
5. Q. takes P. (checkmate).

3. K.'s P. 1.
4. K. moves.

PROBLEM No. 11.

WHITE.

1. B. to Q. B.'s 8th.
2. B. to Q. Kt.'s 8th.
3. Kt. to Q. B.'s 7th.
4. Kt. to K.'s 6th (dis. ch.)
5. Kt. mates, or discovers mate.

BLACK.

1. P. moves.
2. P. moves.
3. K. moves.
4. K. moves or takes P.

PROBLEM No. 12.

WHITE.

1. R. to Q.'s 8th.
2. Q. takes R.
3. P. to R.'s 8th, becomes a Kt.
4. R. takes Kt. at Q.'s 4th.
5. R. to Q.'s 5th (checkmate).

5. Kt. takes B.'s P. (checkmate).

3. R. takes Q.
4. K. takes R.
5. Q. takes Kt.'s P. (checkmate.)

5. R. to Q.'s 5th (checkmate).

3. B. takes Q. B.'s P.
4. P. to K.'s 8th, becomes Kt. or Q.
5. Checkmate.

2. P. to R.'s 8th, becomes Kt.
3. K. takes R.
4. Kt. to B.'s 7th (ch.)
5. Checkmate.

BLACK.

1. Kt. to K. Kt.'s 3rd.
2. Q. takes Q.
3. Kt. takes Kt. (best).
4. P. takes Kt.

If 4. K. takes R., or any other move,

2. R. takes B.
3. R. to R.'s 8th (ch.)
4. P. takes R.

If 4. Any other move.

2. R. to Q. R.'s 2nd.
3. Kt. to R.'s 5th (best).
4. Any move.

1. R. takes B.
2. R. to R.'s 8th (ch.)
3. Q.'s Kt. moves.
4. K. to Q.'s 5th.

There are many subordinate variations to this very interesting problem—the foregoing are the leaders.

PROBLEM No. 13.

WHITE.

1. Q. to K.'s sq. (ch.)
2. Q. to K. Kt.'s sq. (ch.)
3. Q. to K. Kt.'s 7th (ch.)
4. Q. to Q. B.'s 7th (ch.)
5. Kt. to Q. Kt.'s 5th (checkmate).

BLACK.

1. K. to Q.'s 5th (best).
2. K. to K.'s 4th.
3. K. to Q.'s 3rd (best).
4. K. takes Q.

PROBLEM No. 14.

WHITE.

1. B. to K. R.'s 2nd.
2. B. to K. Kt.'s 3rd.
3. B. to K.'s sq.
4. B. takes P.
5. B. takes P.
6. B. to Q. Kt.'s 8th.
7. B. to Q. B.'s 7th.
8. B. to Q. R.'s 5th.
9. B. to Q. B.'s 3rd (checkmate)

BLACK.

1. B. to K.'s 6th.
2. B. to K. Kt.'s 8th.
3. B. to K.'s 6th.
4. B. to Q.'s 7th.
5. B. to Q. Kt.'s 5th.
6. B. to Q. B.'s 4th.
7. B. to Q. R.'s 2nd.
8. Any move.

27*

PROBLEM No. 15.

WHITE.	BLACK.
1. R. to K. B.'s 5th.	1. P. to Q.'s 3rd.
2. B. to K. Kt.'s 5th.	2. P. to R.'s 7th.
3. Q. to Q. R.'s 4th.	3. P. to R.'s 4th.
4. B. to Q. B.'s 2nd.	4. P. to Kt.'s 8th becomes rook
	(best). (a)
5. B. to Q.'s sq. (ch.)	5. R. takes B.
6. Kt. to Q. B.'s sq. (ch.)	6. R. takes Kt.
7. Q. to Q. B.'s 4th (ch.)	7. R. takes Q. (checkmate).

(a) If 4. P. becomes Q. or B.

5. B. to Q.'s 3rd (ch.)   5. Q. or B. takes B. (checkmate).

If 4. P. becomes Kt.

5. Kt. to Q. B.'s 3rd (ch.)   5. Kt. takes Kt. (checkmate).

PROBLEM No. 16.

SOLUTION TO THE "CIRCUS."

WHITE.	BLACK.
1. Kt. to Q.'s 3rd (ch.)	Black's moves are all forced.
2. Kt. to K.'s 3rd (ch.)	
3. Kt. to K. B.'s 4th (ch.)	
4. Kt. to K. B.'s 5th (ch.)	
5. Kt. to K.'s 6th (ch.)	
6. Kt. to Q.'s 6th (ch.)	
7. Kt. to Q. B.'s 5th (ch.)	
8. Kt. to Q. B.'s 4th (ch.)	

And the performance of the horses continues *ad libitum.*

PROBLEM No. 17.

WHITE.	BLACK.
1. Q. to K. R.'s sq.	1. Anything.
2. Q. or R. mates.	

PROBLEM No. 18.

WHITE.	BLACK.
1. R. to K.'s 4th.	1. B. takes R.
2. B. to K. B.'s sq. (checkmate).	

PROBLEM No. 19.

WHITE.	BLACK.
1. Kt. to K. R.'s 4th.	1. K. to Q.'s 4th.
2. Q. to Q.'s 6th (ch.)	2. K. to K.'s 5th.
3. Q. to Q.'s 4th (checkmate).	

PROBLEM No. 20.

WHITE.	BLACK.
1. B. to Q. B.'s sq.	1. Q. Kt. P. 1 or 2 squares.
2. Q. Kt. P. 1, if black plays 2 sqs.; if black plays but 1 sq., then play the P. 2 squares.	2. P. advances.
3. R. to Q.'s 2nd.	3. K. moves.
4. R. to Q.'s 4th (checkmate).	

PROBLEM No. 21.

WHITE.	BLACK.
1. K. to B.'s 2nd.	1. Q. P. 1 (best).
2. B. to K.'s 5th. (ch.)	2. P. takes B.
8 R. to K. R.'s 6th.	3. K. to R.'s 8th.
4. R. takes R. P. (checkmate).	

PROBLEM No. 22.

WHITE.	BLACK.
1. R. takes B. (ch.)	1. P. takes R.
2. Kt. to B.'s 3rd (ch.)	2. K. to K.'s 5th.
8. Kt. to Q.'s 2nd (ch.)	3. K. to B.'s 4th.
4. B. to B.'s 8th (checkmate).	

PROBLEM No. 23.

WHITE.	BLACK.
1. P. to Q. Kt.'s 5th.	1. K. to Q.'s 6th (best).
2. R. to Q.'s 5th (ch.)	2. K. to Q. B.'s 5th.
8. B. to Q. R.'s 4th.	
4 { If K. takes R., B. mates. { If P. moves, R. mates.	

PROBLEM No. 24.

WHITE.	BLACK.
1. Kt. to Q. Kt.'s 4th (dis. ch.)	1. Q. takes R. (best).
2. Q. takes B. (ch.)	2. K. to Q. B.'s 5th.
8. Q. to Q.'s 4th (ch.)	3. P. takes Q.
4. R. to Q. B.'s 7th (checkmate).	

PROBLEM No. 25.

WHITE.	BLACK.
1. B. to Q. Kt.'s 8th.	1. P. to R.'s 3rd (best).
2. B. to K. R.'s 2nd.	2. Kt. to Kt.'s 6th (ch.)
3. Kt. takes Kt. (ch.)	8. K. to B.'s 5th.
4. Kt. to B.'s sq. (ch.)	4. K. to B.'s 4th.
5. Kt. to K.'s 3rd (checkmate).	
	2. Kt. elsewhere.
8. Kt. to Kt.'s 3rd (ch.)	8. K. to B.'s 5th.
4. As above.	4. K. to B.'s 4th.
5. As above (checkmate).	
	8. K. to K.'s 4th.
4. Kt. to K.'s 2nd (ch.)	4. K. to B.'s 4th.
5. Kt. to Q.'s 4th (checkmate).	

PROBLEM No. 26.

WHITE.	BLACK.
1. R. to K. B.'s 2nd.	1. K. moves.
2. B. to K.'s 8th.	2. K. moves.
8. B. to K. B.'s 4th.	8. P. moves.
4. B. to K. R.'s 5th.	4. P. takes B.
5. R. to K.'s 2nd (ch.)	5. K. moves.
6. P. to Kt.'s 5th (dis. mate).	

PROBLEM No. 27.

WHITE.	BLACK.
1. B. to Q. B.'s 5th.	1. P. to R.'s 4th.
2. B. to Q.'s 7th.	2. P. to R.'s 3rd.
3. R. to K. R.'s 8rd.	3. K. to K.'s 4th.
4. R. to K. B.'s 3rd.	4. K. to Q.'s 4th.
5. R. to K. B.'s 5th (checkmate).	

PROBLEM No. 28.

WHITE.	BLACK.
1. Q. to K.'s 4th (ch.)	1. B. takes Q.
2. B. to R.'s sq.	2. Q. to Kt.'s 7th.
3. B. takes Q.	3. B. to B.'s 6th.
4. B. takes R.	4. Moves.
5. P. checkmates. If B. moves, Kt. mates.	

PROBLEM No. 29.

WHITE.	BLACK.
1. Kt. to K. B.'s 5th.	1. B. to Q. Kt.'s 5th.
2. Kt. to Q.'s 8th.	2. B. to Q.'s 3rd.
3. Kt. to K.'s 6th.	3. B. to K.'s 2nd.
4. Kt. to Q. B.'s 7th.	4. B. to Q. B.'s 4th.
5. Kt. to Q.'s 5th.	5. B. moves.
6. Kt. checkmates.	
	1. B. to K.'s 2nd.
2. Kt. to Q. R.'s 5th.	2. B. to Q. B.'s 4th.
3. Kt. to Q. Kt.'s 3rd.	3. B. to Q. Kt.'s 5th or K.'s 6th.
4. Kt. to Q. R.'s sq.	4. B. moves.
5. Kt. to Q. B.'s 2nd.	5. B. moves.
6. Kt. checkmates.	

PROBLEM No. 30.

WHITE.	BLACK.
1. P. takes B. (ch.)	1. P. takes P.
2. R. to R.'s 5th (ch.)	2. Q. interposes.
3. R. at R.'s 5th, takes Q. (ch.)	3. P. takes R.
4. Q. to B.'s 6th (ch.)	4. P. takes Q.
5. B. to K.'s 6th (ch.)	5. P. takes B.
6. R. takes B. (ch.)	6. Kt. interposes.
7. R. takes Kt. (ch.)	7. P. takes R.
8. Kt. checkmates.	

PROBLEM No. 31.

WHITE.	BLACK.
1. Q. to hor 6th.	1. K. to B.'s 2nd.
2. K. R. to R.'s 8th.	2. K. to Kt.'s 2nd.
3. B. to Q. Kt.'s 2nd (ch.)	3. K. to B.'s 2nd.
4. Q. to Q. R.'s 6th.	4. K. to K.'s 2nd.
5. K. B. to K. R.'s 3rd.	5. K. to B.'s 2nd.
6. Q. B. to Q.'s 4th.	6. K. to K.'s 2nd.
7. Q. Kt. to Q. B.'s 3rd.	7. K. to B.'s 2nd.
8. K. Kt. to K. B.'s 3rd.	8. K. to K.'s 2nd.
9. K. to his 2nd.	9. K. to B.'s 2nd.
10. K. to Q.'s 3rd.	10. K. to K.'s 2nd.
11. K. Kt. to Q.'s 2nd.	11. K. to B.'s 2nd.
12. Q. R. to K. Kt.'s sq.	12. K. to K.'s 2nd.
13. Q. Kt. checks.	13. K. to B.'s 2nd.
14. K. R. to K.'s 6th (checkmate).	

Four-handed Chess.

THE game of Chess for four persons is played on a board of one hundred and sixty squares. The following diagram represents the board and men on beginning a game.

B. BLACK MEN.

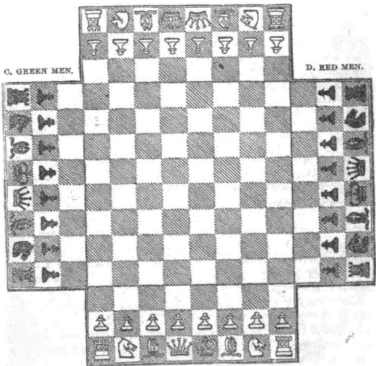

C. GREEN MEN.

D. RED MEN.

A. WHITE MEN.

From this sketch it will be seen that each of the four players has a set of men placed as indicated. We suppose the players to be A, B, C, and D, and that the four colors used are white, black, red, and green. It is right to observe that in all points, excepting such as are here delineated, the game for four is played similar to the usual game for two.

A and B play with the white and black pieces, in partnership, against C and D, to whom are appropriated the green and red. The partners sit opposite to each other.*

The pieces are the same in number, but their position is slightly different, at beginning, to what it is in the ordinary game. The only difference, however, relates to the relative situations of the kings and queens, and this will be best gathered from the foregoing pictured representation. In the game of Chess for two, the kings and queens face each other; but here the king faces the queen, and so on. It is obvious that two of the players will have a white square at their right-hand corner of the board, and two will have a black one. At the beginning of each game, the four players draw lots for the first move.

The move passes round, in turn, always to the left hand; thus, if A play first, C follows; then B, and lastly D. Each player supports and assists his confederate to the utmost, while he opposes the two adverse parties indiscriminately.

The kings of the partners may move on to adjoining squares, and, of course, can go freely into the range of any of their partners' pieces. A queen, or other piece, cannot assume the state of giving check to the partner's king; towards which, as towards her own, all hostile properties lie dormant. This rule equally applies to all the Chess-men.

No player is allowed to move a piece or pawn, the removal of which would open his partner's king to a check from either of the hostile powers, any more than he may uncover his own king to a similar check.

Each player supports his partner in an attack; thus should A put a queen en prise of D's king, unsupported, and should C be unable to take her, or otherwise provide for the check—B may support the queen, and even give mate, in this compound manner.

The pawns can only move one square each time, and not two squares the first move, as in the ordinary game.

It is the general rule to disallow castling, altogether, in the game for four. With some persons, however, it is the custom to adopt it. There being a difference of opinion upon the point, it is best to arrange beforehand respecting it. It is by far the best plan to prohibit castling, as the game is in itself sufficiently complicated.

* The partners are rigorously interdicted, as at Whist, from intimating aught to each other, either by word, look, or gesture.

The pawns do not become pieces, when they reach the opposite end squares of the board; such squares being friendly squares, because in the territory of the partner. But on a pawn's attaining any one of the extreme hostile line of squares, right or left, it becomes a queen. Thus A can only queen a pawn by getting it on to one of the end squares of D or C—such squares being the edge-line of the board. It is evident from this, that a pawn can only queen through making repeated captures; since, unless in the act of taking, it cannot move diagonally.

When a pawn has attained either one of the ultimate squares of the board belonging to your partner, such pawn remains there as a pawn, and moves back again, as a pawn, one square at a time, in the same direction; that is, towards you. A pawn, therefore, which has reached either one of the eight ultimate friendly squares, should be marked in some way to show that it has exchanged its own line of march for a power exclusively of backward motion. Should such pawn return to the line from which it originally started, it moves forward again, as it did at first.

As the partners sit opposite, it sometimes happens that their pawns meet on the board. In every such case, they are allowed to leap over the friendly pawn, and place themselves, on the move, upon the square beyond: always preserving their forward or backward motion, as the case may be, but never leaving their file, save to make a prisoner. The player will soon become accustomed to these little peculiarities.

The game is only won when the two partners are checkmated. Should one be checkmated, and the other be stalemated, the game is drawn, as if both were stalemated.

Should a player be checkmated, his pieces are not removed from the board, but must remain in the same position, his partner continuing the fight single-handed. Of course, while checkmated, he cannot move, and therefore misses his turn. His partner may at any time relieve him, if he can, from the checkmate; in the event of doing which, his pieces regain life, and he again moves in his turn. As, while one is checkmated, the enemy moves twice for once, it is seldom that a checkmate can be relieved, if it has stood more than one move. While a player is in checkmate, his pieces cannot be taken by the adversary, but they remain in the same position. In this case, they present a species of "Caput mortuum," devoid of all offending properties; thus, should the squares be open, the adverse pawns, or pieces, may move between them; going into their check or range with impunity. They still, however, offer the inert resistance of a lifeless mass, by blocking up the squares they actually occupy, &c.

The principle of playing this game well, is in directing the attack to the right hand in preference to the left. For as the move passes round to the left, you thus have the chance of your partner's support. For example, A hav ing to play, attacks D rather than C; being assured, by this, of two hostile moves against D, while the latter, until it is his own turn to play, can only divert the attack by the one intermediate move of his partner C. A skilful player, by thus attacking his right-hand adversary, frequently secures, through the co-operation of his partner, not only the simple capture of a man, but even the giving of checkmate. When you find that your partner, acting on this, has attacked his right-hand adversary, you support him in the best mode you can. In such case, your attack is of course directed against your left-hand adversary, but this attack is rather of a secondary than primary nature, since it does not originate with you.

It would be out of place, in this brief outline of the game, to attempt more than general description. The game of Chess for four is rarely adopted but by tolerably good Chess-players, and it is pretty clear that those who play the common game best, are most likely to excel in this new variety. The game of Chess for four is advancing daily in fashion and favor with the public. It takes in players of every grade; for a good player with a less skilful partner are equally matched against a similar couple; and the less scientific have thus an opportunity of playing in consort with those of greater skill. In so doing, it is believed much instruction is derivable, and it is anticipated that the extension of a knowledge of the game for four, will thus contribute, in no mean degree, to promote the wider diffusion of the finest intellectual recreation yet devised—CHESS.

THE END.

Lightning Source UK Ltd.
Milton Keynes UK
UKHW02f0621180418

321252UK00005B/302/P